These black voices testify to somethin
who were enslaved and oppressed by
Christianity go on to embrace the Ch
speak of the capacity of human nature ... ~~... ... ... and virtue. They
bear witness to the amazing grace of God. Their voices have been kept
silent for too long. On these pages their voices cry and sing, they pray
and preach. The cadences are dignified, the register is noble and the
tone is sombre yet full of hope. Here are true voices of the kingdom.
Rt Revd James Jones, Bishop of Liverpool

At last! An anthology mined from the rich heritage of black British
Christian history. *Black Voices* is a great personal read and an invaluable
resource for further study. I found it stimulating, challenging and
informative. Every educator, preacher and churchgoer should own a
copy.
Revd Dr Kate Coleman, President of the Baptist Union of Great Britain

I very much liked the book – terrific, in fact. I read it at a single sitting.
It is engrossing, readable and an entirely new concept.
Professor James Walvin, University of York; co-editor, Slavery and Abolition

A very moving anthology of writings by people of African descent
who have lived in Britain over the centuries. This book is timely as we
all celebrate the bicentennial of the abolition of the slave trade and also
consider afresh how Britain is to be a diverse but cohesive society in
the twenty-first century. What David and Joel have done for black
people in Britain needs also to be done for Asian and other communities. Who will take up the challenge?
Rt Revd Dr Michael Nazir-Ali, Bishop of Rochester

ivp

Black Voices

The shaping of our Christian experience

David Killingray
Joel Edwards

INTER-VARSITY PRESS
Norton Street, Nottingham NG7 3HR, England
Email: ivp@ivpbooks.com
Website: www.ivpbooks.com

First published 2007

British Library Cataloguing in Publication Data
A catalogue record for this book is available from the British Library.

ISBN: 978–1–84484–181–6

Typeset in Monotype Garamond 11/13pt by CRB Associates, Reepham,
Norfolk, UK
Printed and bound in Great Britain by Ashford Colour Press Ltd,
Gosport, Hampshire

*Inter-Varsity Press publishes Christian books that are true to the Bible and that
communicate the gospel, develop discipleship and strengthen the church for its mission in
the world.*

*Inter-Varsity Press is closely linked with the Universities and Colleges Christian
Fellowship, a student movement connecting Christian Unions in universities and
colleges throughout Great Britain, and a member movement of the International
Fellowship of Evangelical Students. Website: www.uccf.org.uk*

CONTENTS

LIST OF ILLUSTRATIONS

FOREWORD

I warmly recommend *Black Voices* as a welcome contribution to the community of literature which has become part of our educational toolkit in understanding the role of black men and women who have been invisible inspirations to British life in recent centuries.

This book provides an interesting and informative account of the experiences of black Christians who have settled in Britain. It also goes some way in identifying the warm hospitality shown to many, alongside the more widely known rejection and resistance experienced by other black Christians in Britain.

I warmly recommend it to you.

Dr John Sentamu
Archbishop of York

ACKNOWLEDGMENTS

The compilers and editors of historical anthologies owe a great debt to the many people who over the years have recorded in one way or another accounts of their own lives or who have written biographies. In the case of black British Christians no name can be singled out, but this anthology, as is obvious, rests heavily on the work of all of those who have written about the history of black people in Britain, in Africa, and in the Americas. A major debt is to those who have edited and promoted the re-publication of texts long out of print.

There are also individual debts to a number of friends and colleagues who have been generous in giving of their time in reading the text, answering queries, and providing information and illustrations, and who agreed to let us include extracts from books or articles that they have written: Cressida Annesley and Peter Ewart of Canterbury Cathedral Archives, Deborah Breakspear, Iain MacDonald and Constance Mirembe of the London City Mission, Kathy Chater, Christopher Fyfe, Jeffrey Green and Chris Hall of the Baptist Union of Great Britain, Revd Gareth Moody, Sue Mills, the Librarian of the Angus Library at Regent's College Oxford, Paul Scott-Evans and Judy Powles, the Librarian of Spurgeon's College London, Revd Arlington Trottman, Revd Dr Paul Walker, and Prof. James Walvin. We are also grateful to Thomas Williams for photographic help.

We gratefully acknowledge the following publishers and institutions for permission to include extracts and illustrations: London City Mission (illustration on p. 123), Spurgeon's College, London (illustration on p. 27) and St Augustine's Foundation, Canterbury (illustration on p. 117).

PREFACE

Christianity is firmly rooted in history. The Bible is a historical document that tells of God at work in the lives of people in the past, and supremely of the birth, life, death and resurrection of the Lord Jesus Christ, the most important event in human history. For many Christian believers, including some whose conversion narratives appear in this book, the defining point in their lives is when they acknowledge Jesus' death on the cross, experience pardon from the guilt of sin, and then live with God's Holy Spirit within them. It is good for Christians to know how the faith was received by fellow believers in the past, and also to be encouraged by their life and witness.

This anthology looks at the lives and struggles, triumphs and failures, hopes and ambitions of black British Christians over the past 250 years. A few of the figures included are well known; others are not. Our hope is that a wide range of Britons will read this book and discover more about the rich history of the diverse peoples who have populated these islands. At the same time we would like black Christians to find a source of spiritual encouragement, as well as a further dimension to their own history within Britain, in many of these personal accounts. And this history should also be of interest to white Christians who would find in it a new dimension to British and to Christian history rarely mentioned.

What do we mean by 'black' and 'British'? For the purposes

of this anthology our definition of 'black' is restricted to people of African origin and descent. However, what constitutes, or how to define, 'British' identity is a much discussed issue today. For us, and historically, this term embraces those black people who were British subjects and citizens within the changing boundaries of the British Empire, in the Americas, in Africa, and of course within Britain itself. Another qualification for inclusion in the anthology is that the black people arrived in Britain at some time. We have bent the rules a little in a few cases, by according British identity to one or two black people who came from the United States in the nineteenth century but lived in Britain for a number of years. They have become, in our eyes, 'honorary' Britons, as they often thought of Britain as a more welcoming, kindly and hospitable 'home' than their country of birth, where they were either slaves or treated as second-class citizens. Sadly this cannot be said to be the experience of many black people who came to Britain and daily faced prejudice and discrimination.

Where possible we have kept the language and spelling of the original texts. As the writers quoted used different terms and forms to describe their own identity and that of others, we have chosen to spell both 'black' and 'white' in lower case, not privileging one over the other.

THE PRESENCE OF BLACK PEOPLE IN BRITAIN

David Killingray

Today Britain is a multi-ethnic and multicultural country to a much greater extent than ever before in its history. Two hundred and fifty years ago black people were a fairly common sight in the streets of London, particularly in Westminster and the City area, and in major ports such as Liverpool and Bristol, but they were rarely seen throughout the rest of the country. Most worked as servants and artisans, but there were also seaman and other itinerant workers who moved in and out of the country. Probably few of these people were in a position to freely decide whether or not to live here.

In 1770 the black population of Britain may have numbered 10,000–15,000 people, which equates to roughly the same proportion of the population that was black in 1960, but their presence was not as significant. For one thing the status of many, perhaps most, black people in the seventeenth and eighteenth centuries was ambiguous, since they had been brought into Britain as slaves from the colonies or at best as servants by masters who also owned slaves overseas.[1] Few of the black immigrants who came to Britain in the years immediately after 1945 intended to settle permanently in a cold, austere, post-war country. They came to earn wages freely, determined to then return home. However, many stayed in Britain and planted their own presence on the face of British cities and towns. That process was not without its difficulties and challenges; human migration is rarely a smooth process. But the result has been the enriching of British cultural and spiritual life. Black people from different parts of the world, from different cultures and with different languages, have added to the cosmopolitan population which now constitutes modern Britain.

As this anthology is concerned with the voice of black Christians, it is worth pointing out that before the 1950s there were few distinctive black churches in Britain, and those were confined to the port areas of Liverpool, Cardiff, and London's docklands. There were black Christians and black clergy, but they were members and pastors of churches composed overwhelmingly of white Britons. Today the largest churches in Britain are black majority churches, and there are growing denominations established in the last forty years that are overwhelmingly black in leadership and membership.

Black history and black communities
Although Britain had a small black population for several hundred years, that presence has been largely ignored, even by historians. A false but commonly heard view is that Britain's black population dates from as recently as 1950. This idea is only slowly being dented by further research, by slow change to the school curriculum, and events such as the annual 'Black History month'. The past experience of black people in Britain is an integral part of British history; there is no separate black history, although it is possible to pursue that as a particular field of study, in the way that one might take a specific interest in the history of the working classes, women, coal miners, football or the Jewish communities. Like these, the lives and experiences of black people make up part of the rich record of Britain's past.

It is also worth noting that it is less than accurate to talk of the 'black community', even though black people living in a predominantly white society may have certain common or shared experiences. The black population of Britain today, as in the past, is composed of people from a variety of ethnic groups and cultures in Africa and from different countries and islands in the Caribbean. They do not speak the same languages, eat the same food, or understand or even appreciate each others' cultural practices. Some are Muslim, but from many parts of the world; some are Christian; others are non-religious. The black well-educated, professional, middle classes do not live cheek-by-jowl with the black working classes, and have rarely done so. In fact, the divisions that separate other groups of British people also divide black people from one another. Although this book is an anthology of black Christian writing, there is clearly not a single black Christian community in Britain. Denominational and theological differences divide people at certain levels, but there are interests and issues that may also at times draw them close together, as happens with the different Muslim communities.[2]

Many of the people of African origin and descent who came to Britain during the past 250 years – the span of this book – had been or were influenced in some way by the Christian church, by its missions and schools. A good number were active Christians in belief and practice. British religious history flourishes, but a constant complaint by its practitioners is that too often historians of Britain take less account of its significance than its importance demands. The same is true of the history of black Christian activity. Although only a few historians work on the history of black people in Britain, there has been a tendency to ignore the Christian dimension. It is to be hoped that this anthology will help to repair that lack of interest and emphasize the great significance of Christianity in the lives of many black people in Britain's past.

Britain and the transatlantic slave trade

Archaeological and documentary evidence indicates that immigrants from Africa came to live in the British Isles in the period before 1500, for example as soldiers in Roman legions on Hadrian's Wall and in the garrison at York. From the fifteenth century onwards, increasing European contact with Africa, knowledge of and settlement in America and the development of Atlantic commerce all resulted in an increase in the number of Africans coming to Britain.

The growth of the transatlantic slave trade from West Africa to the Americas, a trade managed by both Africans and Europeans, added to the African diaspora. By 1600 hundreds of thousands of Africans, or people of African descent, lived in Asia and the Mediterranean region, as a result of the long-established slave trading systems operating in the predominantly Islamic world. An increasing number of African slaves were also being shipped to Brazil and the

Caribbean, and a few were being landed in North America.
Inevitably some Africans arrived in the British Isles, mainly as
seamen or as slaves brought 'home' by merchants and sea captains,
although there were also black musicians and performers. In
Elizabethan England black people may have numbered several
hundred, particularly in London, and certainly were sufficient in
number for a German merchant to try to gain a royal 'license to take
up so many blackamoores here in this realme and to transport them
into Spain and Portugal' to exchange for English captives held
there.[3]

During the next two centuries the black population of the British
Isles steadily increased as first England's, and then Britain's, empire
grew and British ships came to dominate the Atlantic slave trade in
the eighteenth century. From 1750 until abolition in 1807, British
ships carried nearly 1.9 million slaves across the Atlantic.[4] The ports
of Liverpool, London and Bristol prospered on the brutal traffic
in human beings who were bought in West Africa and shipped in
harsh conditions on the long voyage to the American colonies to be
used as forced labour. It was said of Liverpool that the bricks of
the warehouses that held imported sugar, tobacco, rum and tropical
products had been cemented together by the blood of black
slaves.

Merchants in smaller ports such as Chester, Glasgow, White-
haven, Lancaster and Lyme Regis also sent ships for the risky but
profitable business of slaving in West Africa. And slaving was a
brutal business indeed, although of mutual advantage to both
African and European merchants. Africans were seized, brought
to the coast, and held in barracoons to await sale to a European
ship. This part of the process, conducted by Africans, had a high
death rate. Africans were then sold to Europeans and shipped
across the Atlantic on the 'middle passage' to the American
colonies. Such a voyage took on average nearly nine weeks, but it
could take several months. It was a horrific experience, graphically
described by Olaudah Equiano*.[5] By the time the ship sighted
America more of the slaves had died, and further deaths occurred in
the period known as the 'seasoning', as slaves were sold and
conditioned to a life of servile existence. Altogether well over
half the original number of Africans seized may have died in this

long drawn-out process of securing slaves for labour in America.[6] And few Europeans, or Africans other than the victims, gave much thought to the morality of this trade in men, women and children.

A resulting backwash to this large-scale movement of black people to America, totalling 10–12 million people in the years 1520–1870, was that more black people came to, or were brought to, Britain. They came as seamen, or were brought as servants and labourers, and as slaves. It was common for those who owned estates in the American colonies to bring domestic slaves to Britain as personal servants. A few slaves (English records rarely refer to them as such) of wealthy owners even wore silver collars round their necks as symbols and reminders of their servile status.

In eighteenth-century Britain, when black slaves mixed with white servants, perceptions about status and of 'rights' were inevitably questioned. Ironically some slaves became attached to their owners; for example Jack Beef, brought to Britain from the West Indian island of St Kitts by John Baker, in 1757, was trusted to run errands, including collecting his master's children from school. He moved about fairly freely and also accumulated savings.[7] A few wealthy people owned small black children, usually boys, who were treated as 'pets'; several are depicted in paintings of portraits and family groupings of the seventeenth and eighteenth centuries.[8] Many of these children were discarded or returned to servile and less favoured positions as they grew older and ceased to be a fashion accessory or plaything.

Most black people lived in the major ports of London, Liverpool and Bristol, and in addition there was an itinerant population of black sailors and others.[9] By 1750 black people were also to be found living in every county, many towns, and even in some villages all over the British Isles. It is not known how many black people there were in Britain in total. Contemporary estimates stated there were up to 20,000, but a more careful recent calculation suggests 10,000 black people in London and another 5,000 living in the provinces.[10] The majority were men, with women perhaps constituting 20 per cent of the total black population. Women were often employed as domestic servants,[11] although poverty and misfortune drove a few on to the streets as prostitutes. There were black

women who lived exceptional lives, for example Dido Belle, and
Jane Harry, an accomplished painter, married to a white surgeon
who was a fellow Quaker.[12] Inevitably many black men married
white wives, for example the eighteenth-century Afro-British
writers Olaudah Equiano and Ukawsaw Gronniosaw,*[13] and, in
the early nineteenth century, Samuel Barber.*

A few black men, and even a small number of black women,
were literate and, by good fortune or personal endeavour, were
able to advance themselves socially. One or two had a source of
regular income, could afford to live comfortably, eat well, have
more than one suit, and enjoy leisure time, and thus could be
identified with the 'middling sort' of people. A good example is
Ignatius Sancho,* a shopkeeper in Westminster, a friend of literary
men and painters, entitled by his income to the right to vote.[14]
The former slave Olaudah Equiano mixed with educated white
people and died a relatively wealthy man thanks to the proceeds of
his book. Dido Elizabeth Belle, the black ward of Lord Mansfield,
grew up in his household and received an annuity of £100 in his
will.[15]

In the seventeenth and eighteenth centuries it was widely
recognized in Europe that white people should not be enslaved,
and considerable efforts were made to regain the liberty of captives
in the Muslim states of North Africa, where religion rather than race
often determined servile status.[16] However, in Europe's American
colonies, slavery was largely determined by race and colour.
Africans and Native Americans could be enslaved and owned
legally as chattels, denied the right to marry, separated arbitrarily
from partners and children, denied civil rights and subjected to
harsh punishments. Certainly, there were white people in both
Britain and the colonies who continued to live and work under
terms and conditions that restricted their freedom of movement.
However, unlike black slaves, they could not be bought and sold like
cattle. Black slaves brought to Britain, although they might be legally
chattels in the colonies, were given some legal protection, even if
English law was ambiguous about their freedom. The well-known
chorus of James Thomson's 'Rule, Britannia!', written in 1740,
roared out patriotically in song ever since, defiantly proclaimed that
'Britons never will be slaves'!

So black people could be slaves; white people could also be enslaved by foreign states but should not be! And this meant that skin colour became inevitably a badge of inferiority, marking out black people as belonging to a race that could be enslaved. An early corollary of this was to deny the humanity of black slaves and thus to justify their enslavement. Even when a common humanity was acknowledged, many Europeans, even humanitarians, continued to regard black people as mentally inferior and below them in a hierarchy of humanity. Theological support was never far away. Selective reading of the Bible justified enslaving Africans, and divine approval was sought for both the African slave trade and black slavery. Indeed, some who denounced the slave *trade* and demanded its abolition saw little wrong in the continuation of a system of slavery, provided it was properly regulated and conducted 'humanely'.

The abolition of the slave trade

In the seventeenth and early eighteenth centuries few people questioned the morality of the slave trade. In the 1770s there was a growing demand in both Britain and North America for an end to the trade. The reasons are complex and inter-connected: economic, social and cultural changes associated with industrialization and urbanization, the evangelical revival and 'Enlightenment' ideas that challenged accepted notions of individual worth and productive labour, and rebellion in the British North American colonies encouraged black slaves to flee their masters.[17] American independence severed a transatlantic empire and thus created the circumstances that helped stimulate the campaign in Britain to abolish the slave trade.[18]

The leading abolitionists were overwhelmingly Christians: Quakers, Anglican evangelicals and, a little later, Methodists and Baptists. Their Christian and humanitarian concern was to bring to an end a trade that was brutal and deprived many Africans of their lives and freedoms. One of the first moves was made in London by Granville Sharp, who, in 1772, successfully won a ruling from Chief Justice Mansfield in the Somerset case that a black slave could not be forcibly removed from England and Wales.[19] This legal statement did not actually say that a black person could not be a slave in

England, but it certainly marked the beginning of the end of slavery, as black people increasingly deserted masters and sought other work. A similar case in Scotland in 1778 declared slavery incompatible with Scottish law.[20]

In 1781 Equiano drew Sharp's attention to the case of the slave ship *Zong*, whose master had thrown overboard 131 chained slaves and then claimed their insurance value. Although the subsequent court case failed to bring a conviction, it highlighted the murderous nature of the slave trade and further excited public opinion. The mid-1780s also saw the arrival in Britain of black loyalists, many of them former slaves who had gained their freedom by supporting the British cause in the American revolutionary war, who now swelled the number of the London poor. One solution to this, promoted by the Committee for Relief of the Black Poor, was to send those willing to go as settlers to the new West African colony of Freetown.[21]

For much of the eighteenth century it was unclear whether or not black slaves could be owned in England. The law was not clear, hence the efforts by Sharp to take the cases of black slaves before the courts in the 1760s–70s in order to clarify their legal status. In this period, and up to the 1830s, black people owned as slaves in the colonies continued to be brought to Britain by their owners. Phillis Wheatley,* although an acclaimed and published poet on both sides of the Atlantic, came to Britain as a slave and was manumitted only on her return to America in 1773. Mary Prince* and Ashton Warner* are two other examples of people who were slaves in the colonies but free when they entered Britain in the late 1820s and early 1830s. Many slaves in England, including Equiano, falsely believed that baptism conferred freedom. Black people were baptized, often as adults, most in the Church of England, where their entry into the Christian community is recorded in the parish registers.[22]

In 1787 the Society for Effecting the Abolition of the Slave Trade was founded. Thomas Clarkson travelled the country mobilizing public opinion against the slave trade, while William Wilberforce emerged as the champion of abolition within Parliament. The abolitionist lobby demanded the end of a trade that was seen by many as vital to the national economy and to the economic prosperity of the sugar colonies in the West Indies. Indeed, in the years 1793–1807 slave productivity increased in the West Indian colonies and the wealth derived from the plantation economies grew. Among those who denounced the slave trade were the Afro-British writers Cugoano* and Equiano, both evangelical Christians. Numerous laws after 1788 regulated the conduct of the slave trade, but abolition was achieved only in March 1807.[23]

Emancipation – freeing the slaves

Black slavery continued in the British colonies for another thirty years. Slaves continued to come to Britain, sometimes brought by their owners, as was Mary Prince. Acknowledged as free in the metropole, they reverted to chattels if they returned home to the West Indies, Cape Colony or other parts of the British Empire. The Anti-Slavery Society, re-formed in the years after the French Wars, directed its attention mainly to ending the *foreign* slave trade and for effective policing of Atlantic waters to prevent illegal slaving. In 1823 it renewed the campaign to end slavery in the British Empire. This was successfully achieved, but in two stages, during the 1830s. Formal emancipation was declared by Parliament in 1833, but slaves endured several years of apprenticeship before gaining their freedom in 1838. At the same time slave owners were generously compensated by Britain to the tune of £20 million for their economic loss.

The British and Foreign Anti-Slavery Society campaigned against the system of apprenticeship, for further action to stop the illegal slave trade from Africa, and for an end to slavery in the United States, in other American states and colonies, and also in Africa. The World Anti-Slavery Convention, held in London in June 1840, was attended by two black Christians from Jamaica, Edward Barrett and Henry Beckford.* In the campaign against US slavery, African-Americans, both free people and escaped slaves, spoke to large audiences throughout Britain. The first was Moses Roper* in the 1830s, and he was followed by more than 100 others, including towering figures such as Frederick Douglass and less well-known men and women: Zilpha Elaw,* William and Ellen Craft and Thomas L. Johnson,* all of whom were active Christians. Invariably they found Britain to be a more tolerant and congenial environment than the United States.[24] Many of these African American activists opposed to slavery moved back and forth across the Atlantic, speaking and preaching in Britain and North America. Some became missionaries in Africa and Europe; one or two, for example the Crafts and Johnson, made their homes in Britain.[25]

Throughout the nineteenth century Britain's colonial empire was steadily expanding. London became a crossroads, with people from all parts of the world, including Africa and the Caribbean, coming to the metropole. It has been argued that the black population of Britain declined in the early nineteenth century as the predominantly male black population of the eighteenth century married white wives and this reduced the noticeable number of black people. It is impossible at this stage of research to prove or disprove this. However, it seems more likely that there was a steady inflow of black people into Britain during the first half of the nineteenth century, adding to the number of those already living in the country. As far as can be determined, most were non-literate and worked as servants and labourers; a few found semi-skilled employment. In addition there were sailors, including men who had served in the Royal Navy, along with ex-soldiers demobilized at the end of the war with France.

Education and black elites in nineteenth-century Britain

There were other reasons why black people came to Britain from the colonies. Beginning in the eighteenth century a few West African rulers and traders sent their children to schools in Britain, seeing advantage in their acquiring a good knowledge of English, as well as literacy and numeracy – for example John Naimbanna,* who came from what is now Sierra Leone. In the nineteenth and twentieth centuries elite families in Africa and the Caribbean sent their children, mainly boys but also some girls, to British schools, where their presence and progress can be plotted in school records and publications.[26] Missionary societies and individuals also arranged for young Africans to study in Britain in order to return to Africa as missionaries, one early example being Philip Quaque.*

At the end of the eighteenth century Boston King* studied at the Methodist school at Kingswood, near Bristol. Edward Bickersteth brought the young Simeon Wilhelm* to England for education in 1817, and training 'native agents', as they were called, such as Joseph

Simeon C. Gordon

Calvin Richardson

T.L Johnson

J. McGee

These four men studied at The Pastor's College (now Spurgeon's College) in London between 1867 and 1903.

Wright,* became common practice throughout the nineteenth century.[27] The Church Missionary Society trained African clergy in Islington, for example Samuel Crowther,* the future bishop. The high or Anglo-Catholic part of the Anglican church established St Augustine's College, Canterbury, in 1838, to train clergy for overseas ministry. The College received students from the Eastern Cape, including Gregory Ngcobo* from Zululand, and also Lambert MacKenzie, the first black Caribbean minister to be ordained in the Church of England. The high-church Universities Mission to Central Africa, working in what is now Tanzania, sent Hugh Peter Kayamba to Bloxham School, in Oxfordshire, to complete his secondary education in 1882; on his return home three years later he taught in a mission school.[28] At the end of the century the Colwyn Bay Institute, established in 1888 by a former Welsh Baptist missionary, William Hughes, trained black students for mission work in their homelands.

The Church of England trained black clergy specifically to work overseas, although in the process a few men also briefly ministered in English parishes, for example Alexander Crummell* in Ipswich and Robert Gordon* in East London. Rarely was there a black minister of an English parish; one is known, perhaps uniquely: the Reverend Bryan Mackey, from Kingston, Jamaica, who was rector of Coates in Gloucestershire from 1799 to 1847.[29] Itinerant black preachers were common in nineteenth-century Britain, including women such as Zilpha Elaw and Amanda Smith.* Many clergymen, both Anglican and nonconformist, welcomed black visitors to speak in their churches on special occasions, especially if they were ordained or missionaries. More interesting for what it may tell us about attitudes to race in the nineteenth century are those white congregations in Baptist churches in Aylesbury, the West Midlands, Sussex, London and Hertfordshire which invited a black minister to become their pastor.[30] John Jea* was minister of a church in Portsea sometime in the early nineteenth century, presumably one with a predominantly white congregation. Black preachers were of all sorts: there was the respectable, reasoned debater like S. J. Celestine Edwards,* who preached in an East London park and ran a weekly men's Bible class; the rabidly anti-Roman Catholic rabble-rouser John S. Orr, who excited violence wherever he went in Britain, North America, or his home colony of British Guiana; evangelists with a passionate gospel message sustained by a gripping personal story of adversity, hardship and struggle (David George,* George Liele,* Thomas L. Johnston, and James Newby*) and the Gold Coast businessman T. Brem Wilson, who established a Pentecostal meeting in London in 1906.[31] From 1920 to 1946 probably the most active black lay preacher was Dr Harold Moody,* whose sermons and talks, in which he often referred to the curse of racial discrimination, were heard by thousands of white people up and down the country. By the late twentieth century, black clergy, both men and women, were common in most denominations, although not the Roman Catholic Church,[32] and black missionaries were working in Britain's major cities, for example Constance Mirembe* in London.

The quest for a modern formal education, the need for clergy training, and personal ambition to gain professional qualifications,

𝕮𝖍𝖊 𝕷𝖆𝖙𝖊 𝕸𝖗. 𝕵𝖔𝖍𝖓 𝕻𝖎𝖕𝖊𝖗,

BAPTIST MINISTER.

"Death is swallowed up in victory."—1 Cor. xv. 54.

John Piper was born in the colony of British Guiana. He became an itinerant Baptist preacher in England and was later minister of a church in St Albans. He died there and is buried in the local cemetery. None of his sermons is known to have survived; perhaps one will be found eventually!

resulted in a steady stream of black students coming to the handful of British universities to study from the 1850s onwards.[33] As the crossroads of a growing Empire, Britain regularly received black visitors and settlers from the colonies. People came for a variety of reasons: diplomats, traders, entertainers, servants, seamen, labourers, campaigners against slavery, journalists, students, preachers, and evangelists arrived in Britain with purpose or as a result of circumstance.[34] Some stayed briefly, others for a specific time and purpose such as study, while a few settled, often marrying white Britons.

Areas of London, Liverpool and Bristol continued to have small black-minority populations, and others also developed in Cardiff's Bute town from the 1850s, and in South Shields after 1900, mainly as a result of seaman settlers.[35] It is important to stress that a small but increasing and significant part of the black population, especially in London, was composed of professional men and women, many of whom had received an education at a higher level than the average middle-class white Briton. Many were graduates of Scottish or English universities, often earning further professional qualifications, and some wrote books that were published in Britain.[36]

Local responses by white Britons to black people varied considerably. One or two black people in a community might attract little attention; a larger number, especially if men, might be viewed as a threat to housing, to jobs, and as rivals for white female affection. The picture from the years before 1860 is patchy. During that decade and after, race and colour appear to become more significant in British popular thinking and stereotypical ideas of black people became more rigidly fixed. 'Scientific racist' ideas propounded by ethnographers, Darwin's theories of natural selection promoted by those who focused on race, and the expansion of overseas empire, especially in Africa after 1880, all helped promote new notions of white racial superiority and hardened opinions as to the nature and quality of black people.[37]

The twentieth century

By 1911 there may have been 10,000–12,000 black people living in Britain. The precise figure is unknown. During and immediately after the First World War, when black people came to Britain to join the armed forces and as labour, the black population may have reached 20,000. In the straitened economic climate of 1919 there were outbursts of white working-class hostility towards black people in various British cities, most notably in Liverpool and Cardiff.[38] Twenty-two years earlier black people in Britain had formed an organization to represent their pan-African interests. This led to the Pan-African Conference of 1900, held in London, although little came from this international gathering at the time.[39] However, it followed an earlier political path marked by men such as Equiano, who campaigned against the slave trade and was a member of the radical London Corresponding Society, and Robert Wedderburn who embraced Christianity but became a unitarian and then a radical freethinker with his own chapel in London's Soho.[40]

Black-owned and black-edited journals and newspapers also appeared in the early twentieth century, but with a limited circulation and based on weak finances.[41] Nevertheless, they voiced black people's ideas and activities, in particular the demands of the delegations led by Sol Plaatje* that the British government protect 'native rights' in South Africa. Meanwhile a few black people had been elected to political office in local government, most notably John Archer, who became mayor of Battersea in 1913. Black-led organizations were also formed, among the first being the West African Students' Christian Union in universities. Some of these students helped to organize the African Progress Union and the Society of Peoples of African Origin in 1918–20, political bodies that were brought together mainly by the efforts of Felix Hercules.*

In the 1920s the West African Student Union was formed (it issued a journal, *WASU*), and six years later, in 1931, Harold Moody,* a Christian doctor with a practice in South London, helped found the League of Coloured Peoples (LCP), a black-led but multiracial body that campaigned against the officially endorsed and privately practised racism that was endemic in Britain.[42] Over the next ten years the LCP became politically more radical and also the most significant black-led body in Britain, although Moody's leadership was criticized for being too passive by Marxists and left-wing radicals such as C. L. R. James and George Padmore. With Moody's death in 1947, the LCP steadily lost influence. At a time when an increasing number of black immigrants was entering Britain, the black-led organizations were relatively weak and ineffective in opposing the rising tide of white racism.

This racism became more pronounced during the Second World War. Britain's black population increased, with men and women coming from the Caribbean and Africa to join the armed forces and to work for the war effort. From 1942 to 1945 the black population of Britain rapidly grew to its largest number ever due to the presence of 120,000 black GIs from the United States. The US forces brought into Britain not only many white soldiers with racist attitudes, but also its institutionalized discriminatory policies and practices. Inevitably racial tension increased, with some of the most serious abuse and conflict caused by white US soldiers and directed against black British citizens. Racial tension increased and black British citizens and subjects experienced increased racial abuse and discrimination.

At the end of the war, Britain was faced with a labour shortage and was only too grateful to import black workers from the Caribbean. A new chapter in the history of Britain's black population was marked by the arrival of nearly 500 black workers, mainly men, from the Caribbean on the *Empire Windrush* in mid-1948. Many of these men were skilled and were returning to Britain, where they had worked during the war years. Faced with a continued labour shortage, men and women from the Caribbean were encouraged to come to work in Britain throughout the 1950s, their right of entry being guaranteed because they were British subjects. However, rising numbers of black immigrants (although substantially fewer in number than white immigrants from Europe), and their concentration in certain regions of the country and areas of towns, met with an angry response from some white people and politicians, who demanded a control on non-white immigration. The government bowed to this pressure and in 1962 introduced the restrictive and racially weighted Commonwealth Immigrants Act, but not before many dependants of those who were working in Britain had availed themselves of the opportunity to enter the country. The result was a steep increase in black immigration in the years 1958–62.[43]

Since then the black population has steadily increased by natural growth and, since the 1970s, by entry into the country of Africans fleeing the political unrest and economic disruption within their continent. Britain received more white immigrants than blacks in these decades, although clearly their presence has not been so visually obvious. The contribution of black Britons to this country has been enormous. Many vital public services from schools to hospitals would not function without them. Their cultural and Christian impact has been significant and substantial.

The black Christian contribution
There is much that is not known about the history of the black population of Britain in the last 400 years. Predictably, more is known about the years since 1770, not only because it is more recent

and there are more sources, but also because black people wrote books and contributed to journals and newspapers in that period. As many of the literate black people who came to Britain were Christians or from Christian backgrounds, it is not surprising that references to them can be found in the burgeoning religious press and publications that were widely read in the nineteenth century. Historians working on the history of black people have profitably used local newspapers, but relatively few have looked at the archives, newspapers, journals, and other publications of the different Christian denominations and churches and the domestic and foreign missionary societies.[44]

The history of the black Christian experience in Britain has yet to be written. Given the paucity of research as yet, it is perhaps too early to embark on such a venture. The recorded voices of black Christians represented in this anthology are but a small proportion of the total. Most people do not write about their lives and experiences. The vast majority of black Christians lived quiet, ordinary lives and rarely thought that their activities were worthy of record. And yet some had remarkable histories to tell, for example Dr Christopher J. Davis, from West Africa, who studied medicine at Aberdeen, where he belonged to a local Christian Brethren meeting and did mission work among local people; he died of disease at Sedan while helping wounded soldiers during the Franco-Prussian war of 1870.[45] Or Isaac Dickerson, a member of the Fisk University Jubilee Singers who toured Britain in the 1870s and sang at the Moody and Sankey revival meetings, who studied in Scotland, became a missionary in France and died in south-east London in 1900. Churches and Christian organizations often kept records of the activities of ordinary members in minute books and reports, and further information on black Christians can be gleaned from denominational newspapers and magazines.

The majority of black Christians, whether from the Caribbean since 1950, or from Africa in the decades since 1970, have been Protestant. The early independent black churches, mainly Pentecostal, soon created denominations such as the Calvary Church of God in Christ and the New Testament Church of God. Many of the African churches were branches of those already existing in Africa; some were theologically orthodox while others were not, their doctrines being a mix of African indigenous beliefs and selected Christian doctrines. Many churches of African origin were dominated by a single leader; a number of these churches were very large, for example Matthew Ashimolowo's Kingsway Christian International Centre in London, having over 5,000 members. One of the most significant developments in black majority churches has been new forms of music, which have had an impact in many white majority churches.

From the 1970s, the black majority churches began to forge closer links with other churches, and also to co-ordinate approaches to local and central government and welfare institutions in activities relating to housing, education, youth work and childcare. In 1979 Oli Abiola helped form the Council of African and African Caribbean Churches in an attempt to gain recognition from the British Council of Churches for the African spiritual and independent churches. A few years later, Philip Mohabir created the African and Caribbean Evangelical Alliance (ACAE), which sought to bridge the gap between black and white evangelicals.

Although many black immigrants found the fellowship and form of white-majority churches unwelcoming, so that they formed their own churches, some black Christians, especially Anglicans, remained within that communion. Black-majority Anglican churches existed in certain urban areas of England, and black clergy advanced up the hierarchy, Wilfred Wood to be the Bishop of Croydon, and John Sentamu to proceed from the see of Stepney via Birmingham to become Archbishop of York in 2005. Joel Edwards, a member of the New Testament Church of God, moved from the ACEA to become General Director of the Evangelical Alliance, a body whose members were mainly white-majority churches.

For a long time black Christians were not active in politics, but this changed after 1980. In 1998 David Muir founded the Black Christian Civic Forum to encourage black-majority churches to become politically active. Long before that, Sam King* had been elected the Labour mayor of Southwark, and Paul Boateng* and Baroness Patricia Scotland had become Labour government ministers, while John Taylor, rejected as a candidate in the safe Conservative seat of Cheltenham, had been appointed a Tory peer in the House of Lords. Black Christians and black-majority churches by the early twenty-first century were beginning to make their presence felt and heard. Black Christians were no longer isolated individuals in a sea of racial suspicion, as they had been a century before. Now they had institutions that gave them influence, well-known leaders who gave them much more confidence in public and social affairs, and, most importantly, the ability better to proclaim the message of salvation through Jesus Christ to an increasingly sceptical and secular age.

Notes

1. Despite being written over twenty years ago, the best introduction to the history of black people in Britain is by Peter Fryer, *Staying Power: The History of Black People in Britain* (London, 1984).

2. J. D. Aldred, *Respect: Understanding Caribbean British Christianity* (Peterborough, 2005), provides a good discussion on this matter.

3. Miranda Kaufman, ' "The speedy transportation of blackamoores": Caspar Van Senden's search for Africans and profit in Elizabethan England', *Black and Asian Studies Association Newsletter* 45 (April 2006), pp. 10–14. This corrects the interpretation, frequently stated, that the Elizabethan state officially tried to expel black people from England; e.g. see Fryer, *Staying Power*, pp. 10–12.

4. David Richardson, 'The British Empire and the Atlantic slave trade, 1660–1807', in P. J. Marshall, ed., *The Oxford History of the British Empire* 2: *The Eighteenth Century* (Oxford, 1998), pp. 44–64.

5. Olaudah Equiano, *The Interesting Narrative of the life of Olaudah Equiano or Gustavus Vassa, the African* (London, 1789). In this introduction, an asterisk next to a person's name indicates that he or she is included in the anthology.

6. James Walvin, *Black Ivory: A History of British Slavery* (London, 1992); Hugh Thomas, *The Slave Trade: The History of the Atlantic Slave Trade 1440–1870* (London, 1997); Herbert S. Klein, *The Atlantic Slave Trade* (Cambridge, 1999).

7. Philip C. Yorke, ed., *The Diary of John Baker* (London, 1931). Jack Beef even rode to hounds. He was freed in 1771 but died suddenly just before he was to return to the Caribbean.

8. See Jan Marsh, ed., *Black Victorians: Black People in British Art 1800–1900* (London, 2005).

9. Emma Christopher, *Slave Ship Sailors and Their Captive Cargoes 1730–1807* (Cambridge, 2006).

10. Kathy Chater, 'Untold Histories: Black People in England During the British Slave Trade, 1660–1807' (PhD thesis, University of London, forthcoming), whose more extensive research modifies the numbers given by Norma Myers, *Reconstructing the Past: Blacks in Britain 1780–1830* (London, 1996), ch. 2.

11. For example Frances (Fanny) Coker, 1767–1820, a former slave, who became a member of Broadmead Baptist Church, Bristol, in 1789; see Christine Eickelman's entry in H. C. G. Matthew and Brian Harrison, eds., *The Oxford Dictionary of National Biography* (Oxford, 2004), 12, pp. 481–2.

12. See Judith Jennings, *Gender, Religion, and Radicalism in the Long Eighteenth Century. The 'Ingenious Quaker' and Her Connections* (Aldershot, 2006), pp. 54–59, 74, 82–83, 88–89; also Joseph J. Green, 'Jenny Harry, later Thresher (c. 1756–1784)', *Friends Quarterly Examiner* (1913), pp. 559–582, and (1914), pp. 43–63.

13. *A Narrative of the most remarkable particulars in the life of James Albert Ukawsaw Gronniosaw, An African prince, as related by himself* (Bath, 1772).

14. Ignatuis Sancho, *Letters of the late Ignatius Sancho, an African. In two volumes To which are attached memoirs of his life* (London, 1782). Reyahn King et al., *Ignatius Sancho: An African Man of Letters* (London, 1997).

15. Gretchen Gerzina, *Black England: Life Before Emancipation* (London, 1995).

16. White captives were enslaved and harshly treated in North African states; this was the lot of Robinson Crusoe in Daniel Defoe's eponymous novel (1719). Most Europeans thought the enslavement of whites to be unjust and great efforts were made diplomatically and by community action to redeem them. See Linda Colley, *Captives: Britain, Empire and the World 1600–1850* (London, 2002); Robert C. Davis, *Christian Slaves and Muslim Masters: White Slavery in the Mediterranean, the Barbary Coast and Italy 1500–1800* (Basingstoke, 2003); Gilles Milton, *White Gold: The Extraordinary Story of Thomas Pellow and North Africa's One Million European Slaves* (London, 2004).

17. See Gary B. Nash, *The Forgotten Fifth: African Americans in the Age of Revolution* (Cambridge, MA, 2006), ch. 1.

18. On this last point see Christopher Leslie Brown, *Moral Capital: Foundations of British Abolitionism* (Chapel Hill, NC, 2006).

19. Steven M. Wise, *Though the Heavens May Fall: The Landmark Trial That Led to the End of Human Slavery* (New York, 2005).

20. Iain Whyte, *Scotland and the Abolition of Black Slavery 1756–1838* (Edinburgh, 2006).

21. Stephen J. Braidwood, *Black Poor and White Philanthropists: London's Blacks and the Foundation of the Sierra Leone Settlement 1786–1791* (Liverpool, 1994). See also Norma Myers, 'Servant, sailor, soldier, tailor, beggarman: black survival in white society 1780–1830', *Immigrants and Minorities* 12.1 (1993), pp. 47–74.

22. Parish registers recording baptisms, marriages, and burials in England date from 1538. Many of these baptisms were of young people or adults.

23. Christopher Leslie Brown, 'From slaves to subjects: envisioning an Empire without slavery, 1772–1834', in Philip D. Morgan and Sean Hawkins, eds., *Black Experience and the Empire* (Oxford, 2005), pp. 111–140. David Brion Davis, *The Problem of Slavery in the Age of Revolution 1770–1823* (New York, 1999). Roger Anstey, *The Atlantic Slave Trade and British Abolition 1760–1810* (London, 1975).

24. Ellen Craft said, 'I had much rather starve in England, a free woman, than be a slave for the best man that ever breathed upon the American continent.' Quoted by Carter G. Woodson, *The Mind of the Negro* (Washington, DC, 1926).

25. The United States ended slavery in 1865 following a bloody civil war; Brazil abolished slavery in 1888.

26. See Christopher Fyfe, 'Sierra Leoneans in English schools in the nineteenth century', in Rainer Lotz and Ian Pegg, eds., *Under the Imperial Carpet: Essays in Black History 1780–1950* (Crawley, 1986), pp. 25–31. David Killingray, 'Africans in the United Kingdom: an introduction', in Killingray, ed., *Africans in Britain* (London, 1994), pp. 2–27.

27. Bickersteth's *Memoirs of Simeon Wilhelm* (1819) was a story of a young pious Christian life intended as an example to other Christians. Black people frequently featured in this kind of literature, for example Legh Richmond's *Annals of the Poor: The Negro Servant* (London, c. 1809), and *The African Stranger*, in the Cottage Library of Christian Knowledge (London, n.d., c. 1810). Wilson Armistead, *A Tribute for the Negro* (Manchester, 1848), contains biographies of Christian men and women who are held up as exemplars of black achievement and piety.

28. Margery Perham, ed., *Ten Africans: A Collection of Life Stories* (London, 1936), p. 174.

29. J. Ayres, ed., *Paupers and Pig Killers: The Diary of William Holland, a Somerset Parson 1799–1818* (Stroud, 1984), p. 106.

30. See Killingray, 'Black Baptists', pp. 77–79. Also Killingray, 'Black evangelicals in darkest Britain 1780s–1930s', in Mark Smith, ed., *British Evangelical Identities: Past, Present and Possible Futures*, 1: *History and Sociology* (Carlisle, forthcoming).

31. Desmond Cartwright, 'From the back streets of Brixton to the Royal Albert Hall: British Pentecostalism 1907–1926', unpublished paper given at the 1st meeting of the European Pentecostal Theological Association, Leuven, Belgium, 28–29 December 1981.

32. This anthology contains a single black Roman Catholic, Learie Constantine, and he admitted that he parted from that church. Dr John Alcindor, from Trinidad, was a devoted and active Christian and Catholic; see Jeffrey Green, 'John Alcindor (1873–1924): a migrant's biography', *Immigrants and Minorities* 6.2 (1987). See also Green, *Black Edwardians: Black People in Britain 1901–1914* (London, 1998), ch. 10, 'In the service of their Lord'.

33. See the chapters by David Killingray, Hakim Adi, John D. Hargreaves, and Anthony Kirk-Greene, in Killingray, ed., *Africans in Britain* (London, 1994). Also Ray Jenkins, 'Gold Coasters overseas, 1880–1919: with specific reference to their activities in Britain', *Immigrants and Minorities* 4.3, (1985), pp. 5–25. The education in Britain of a West African woman can be followed in Adelaide M. Cromwell, *An African Woman Feminist: The Life and Times of Adelaide Smith Casely Hayford 1868–1960* (Washington, DC, 1992), ch. 3.

34. Research on Britain's nineteenth-century black population proceeds slowly, made difficult by the scattered and sparse nature of the records. The official decennial Census Enumerators' reports, from 1851 onwards, do not indicate the race or colour of individuals, only the place of birth.

35. For a recent general survey see Winston James, 'The Black experience in twentieth-century Britain', in Philip D. Morgan and Sean Hawkins, eds., *Black Experience and the Empire* (Oxford, 2004), ch. 12. More specifically, see Kenneth Little, *Negroes in Britain: A Study of Racial Relations in English Society* (London, 1948; revised edn 1972), Part I, 'The coloured people of Cardiff'; Alan Llywd, *Cymru Ddu Black Wales: A History* (Cardiff, 2005); Diane Frost, *Work and Community Among West African Migrant Workers Since the Nineteenth Century* (Liverpool, 1999), on Liverpool; Richard I. Lawless, *From Ta'izz to Tyneside: An Arab Community in the North-east During the Early Twentieth Century* (Exeter, 1995), on South Shields, which also included

Somalis; Michael Banton, *The Coloured Quarter: Negro Immigrants in an English City* (London, 1955), on East London; Ian Grosvenor, Rita McLean, and Siân Roberts, eds., *Making Connections Birmingham Black International History* (Birmingham, 2004).

36. The literary record of black Britons is impressive, starting with the late eighteenth-century Afro-British writers. Books by African American opponents of slavery were widely published and read in mid-nineteenth-century Britain. Black writers, mainly from Africa, in the years after 1850, wrote books on medicine, travel, languages, ethnography, politics, religion, as well as novels and poetry.

37. See Philip D. Curtin, *The Image of Africa: British Ideas and Action 1780–1850* (London, 1965); Christine Bolt, *Victorian Attitudes to Race* (London, 1971); Douglas A. Lorimer, *Colour, Class and the Victorians: English Attitudes to the Negro in the Mid-Nineteenth Century* (Leicester, 1978); Shearer West, *The Victorians and Race* (London, 1996) and Paul Rich, *Race and Empire in British Politics* (Cambridge, 2nd edn, 1990).

38. Jacqueline Jenkinson, 'The 1919 race riots in Britain: a survey', in Lotz and Pegg, *Under the Imperial Carpet*, pp. 182–207.

39. The most useful book on pan-Africanism, although published nearly forty years ago, is still Imanuel Geiss, *The Pan-African Movement* (German edn, 1968; London, 1974). On the 1900 Conference see Jonathan Schneer, *London 1900: The Imperial Metropolis* (New Haven, 1999), ch. 9.

40. For Wedderburn (1762–1835) see Iain McCalman, ed., *The Horrors of Slavery and Other Writings by Robert Wedderburn* (Edinburgh, 1991).

41. *The Telephone*, edited by John Edward Quinlan for his National Society for the Protection of the Dark Races, produced one issue in 1907; Dusé Mohamed Ali's *African Times and Oriental Review* ran from 1913/14 to 1918/20, and John Eldred Taylor's *African Telegraph* for a similar period.

42. Hakim Adi, *West Africans in Britain 1900–1960* (London, 1998). Roderick Macdonald, 'Dr. Harold Moody and the League of Coloured People, 1931–1947: a retrospective view', *Race* 14.3 (1975), pp. 291–310; David Killingray, ' "To do something for the race": Harold Moody and the League of Coloured Peoples', in Bill Schwarz, ed., *West Indian Intellectuals in Britain* (Manchester, 2003), pp. 51–70.

43. There are many studies on Britain's post-war immigration policy; see Ian R. G. Spencer, *British Immigration Policy Since 1939: The Making of Multi-racial Britain* (London, 1997).

44. For example, Harold Moody became national president of Christian Endeavour in 1936 and his speeches and activities on behalf of the Union are recorded in the weekly *Christian Endeavour Times*.

45. See obituary in *The Aberdeen Free Press*, 9 December 1870, and John D. Hargreaves, 'The good black doctor: Christopher J. Davis, 1840–1870', *ASACHIB Newsletter* (London) 16 (1996), pp. 6–7.

1. CONVERSION

PHILLIS WHEATLEY c. 1753–84: Providence in adversity?
Phillis Wheatley was born in West Africa, but taken to Boston on a slave ship called *Phillis* in 1761. She was bought by John and Susanna Wheatley (he was a Boston merchant) and employed as a domestic servant. Phillis learned to read and her precocious talent for writing poetry was encouraged by her mistress. Some of her poems were published in Boston newspapers. It was not uncommon for Christian slaves and free blacks in the Americas to describe their forced removal from Africa to America as being in God's providential plan, which Phillis does in this poem. (See also pp. 57, 74.)

On being brought from AFRICA to AMERICA.

'TWAS mercy brought me from my *Pagan* land,
Taught my benighted soul to understand
That there's a God, that there's a *Saviour* too:
Once I redemption neither sought nor knew.
Some view our sable race with scornful eye,
'Their colour is a diabolic die.'

Phillis Wheatley, the poet. This engraving shows Phillis in thoughtful, creative mood. Reproduced from *Poems on Various Subjects, Religious and Moral* (1773).

> Remember, *Christians, Negros*, black as *Cain*,
> May be refin'd, and join th' angelic train.

Source: Phillis Wheatley, *Poems on Various Subjects, Religious and Moral* (London, 1773), p. 18.
See further: *Phillis Wheatley: Complete Works*, ed. Vincent Carretta (London, 2001).

JAMES ALBERT UKAWSAW GRONNIOSAW c. 1730–?:
A slave conversion

Gronniosaw was born in what is now northern Nigeria. In his *Narrative*, published in Bath in 1772, he describes how he was enslaved and taken first to the West Indies and then to North America. His owner there was Theodorus Frelinghuysen, a Reformed Dutch minister and friend of Jonathan Edwards[1] and

George Whitefield.[2] Gronniosaw was sent to school and his owner gave him a copy of Richard Baxter's *A Call to the Unconverted*;[3] reading this book led to his conversion. (See also pp. 139–140.)

> I was one day in a most delightful frame of mind; my heart so overflowed with love and gratitude to the Author of all my comforts. – I was so drawn out of myself, and so fill'd and awed by the Presence of God that I saw (or thought I saw) light inexpressible dart down from heaven upon me, and shone around me for the space of a minute. – I continued on my knees, and joy unspeakable took possession of my soul. – The peace and serenity which filled my mind after this was wonderful, and cannot be told. – I would not have changed situations, or been any one but myself for the world. I blessed God for my poverty, that I had no worldly riches or grandeur to draw my heart from Him ... I seemed to possess a full assurance that my sins were forgiven me. I went home all my way rejoicing ... The first opportunity that presented itself, I went to my old school-master, and made known to him the happy state of my soul who joined with me in praise to God for his mercy to me the vilest of sinners.

Source: *A Narrative of the Most Remarkable Particulars in the Life of James Albert Ukawsaw Gronniosaw, An African Prince, As Related by Himself* (Bath, 1772), pp. 25–26.
See further: Vincent Carretta, *Unchained Voices: An Anthology of Black Authors in the English-Speaking World of the 18th Century* (Lexington, 1996), pp. 32–58.

OLAUDAH EQUIANO c. 1745–97:
Coming to faith in Jesus Christ
Olaudah Equiano wrote a two-volume autobiography, published in 1789, in which he describes his childhood in southern Nigeria, and how he was stolen as a child and sold into slavery first in Africa and then taken to the Americas. In 1766 Equiano bought his freedom, came to Britain, and worked as a seaman. Chapter 10 of his autobiography has the heading, 'Some account of the manner of the author's conversion to the Faith of Jesus Christ'. This describes how he thought that by living a good life he could earn God's favour but this belief gave him no comfort. In his words, he did 'wrestle' with God. (See also pp. 78–82.)

... As I was reading and meditating ... and reflecting on my past actions, I began to think I had lived a moral life, and that I had a proper ground to believe I had an interest in the divine favour; but still meditating on the subject, not knowing whether salvation was to be had partly for our own good deeds, or solely as the sovereign gift of God: – in this deep consternation the Lord was pleased to break in upon my soul with his bright beams of heavenly light; and in an instant, as it were, removing the veil, and letting light into a dark place, Isaiah xxv.7. I saw clearly, with the eye of faith, the crucified Saviour bleeding on the cross on Mount Calvary: the Scriptures became an unsealed book, I saw myself a condemned criminal under the law, which came with its full force to my conscience, and when 'the commandment came sin revived, and I died.' I saw the Lord Jesus Christ in his humiliation loaded and bearing my reproach, sin, and shame. I then clearly perceived, that by the deed of law no flesh living could be justified. I was then convinced, that by the first Adam sin came, and by the second Adam (the Lord Jesus Christ) all that are saved must be made alive. It was given me at that time to know what it was to be born again, John iii.5 ... When I considered my poor wretched state, I wept, seeing what a great debtor I was to sovereign free grace. Now the Ethiopian was willing to be saved by Jesus Christ, the sinner's only surety, and also to rely on none other person or thing for salvation ... Oh! The amazing things of that hour can never be told – it was joy in the Holy Ghost!

Source: Olaudah Equiano, *The Interesting Narrative of The Life of Olaudah Equiano, or Gustavus Vassa, The African. Written by Himself* (London, 1789; 1794 edn), pp. 283–85.
See further: *Olaudah Equiano: The Interesting Narrative and Other Writings*, ed. Vincent Carretta (London, 1995); Vincent Carretta, *Equiano the African: Biography of a Self-Made Man* (Athens, GA, and London, 2005).

THE ENSLAVED AFRICAN PRINCES 1767–72:
Believing in the 'Creator of the World'
In 1767 two young West Africans, Little Ephraim Robin John and Ancona Robin John, who were slavers, were betrayed by African competitors and sold to a British slave ship. Both men were taken to

the Caribbean. As they spoke English they succeeded in getting themselves first to Virginia and then, in 1772, to Bristol. Although they were still slaves, Chief Justice Lord Mansfield[4] had recently delivered a legal decision which stated that slaves could not be forcibly removed from England. Little Ephraim heard of this and he appealed to Lord Mansfield. While in Bristol the two Africans learned to read, lived with Methodists and were particularly close to Charles Wesley[5] and his family. Both Little Ephraim and Ancona Robin became Christians and were baptized by Wesley. When they eventually gained their freedom they returned to their home in Old Calabar and, despite their experiences and their continued Christian beliefs, resumed the buying and selling of slaves.

In appealing to Lord Mansfield, the two men said:

> We, Little Ephraim Robin-John and Ancona Robin John, believing in One God, the Creator of the world, and that God is a rewarder of them that do well, and an avenger of those that do ill ...

In August 1773, Little Ephraim wrote to Charles Wesley:

> Your Brother [John] has been so kind as to talk to us and has given us the Sacrament thrice[.] I find him so good as he shew me when I do wrong[.] I feel in my heart great trouble & see great deal more of my faults & the faults of my Countrymen which I hope the Lord will permit me to tell them when I come home.

In September 1774, as the two Africans were due to sail for West Africa, they wrote to Charles Wesley, addressing him as 'My Dear Charles'. Ancona Robin wrote:

> I fear this be the last I shall be able to write to you ... you have bin so good to us that we can never thank you enough for your love to us but now we must take our Leave with Litting [letting] you know how kind our Bristol friends have been to us ... we had a very Blessed time last night with Mr. [John] Wesley[6] who offered us up in a very solemn manner to God and we Humbly hope his prayer will be heard[.] I must conclude with kindest love to all.

Source: Randy J. Sparks, *The Two Princes of Calabar: An Eighteenth-Century Atlantic Odyssey* (Cambridge, MA, 2004), pp. 114, 125, 132.

ANN DUCK 1717–44: Repentance?

Ann was born in Surrey to a black father and white mother, both domestic servants. The family moved to London. Ann was a good child; she learned to read, write and do accounts, and at about the age of twelve she was employed in a shop. When her father died in 1740, Ann's behaviour changed. She became a prostitute and a member of a criminal gang, the Black Boy Alley Crew. Ann was arrested, tried at the Old Bailey, and sentenced to death. In this letter, supposedly written by Ann to her mother, she confesses her wild life, repentance and trust in Christ. Whether she actually wrote the letter is unclear; it is typical of letters written by some condemned prisoners. Perhaps this shows Ann Duck's genuine repentance. Two days later she was hanged at Tyburn.

> Honoured Mother,
> My Trust being in the Divine Mercies of God Almighty, through the Merits of my Blessed Saviour Jesus Christ whose precious Blood was shed on the Cross for lost and undone Sinners – Glory be to the Holy Names – seeing there were no other Means better to bring me to Himself, than by this Sort of Death – O Lord, I thank and praise thy Holy Name, for all thy Mercies – O lord, if I had lived on in my former Course, I might have died as a Brute Beast, having neither Sense of thy Mercies, nor my having a Soul, which is thy Property: thou gave it and to Thee, O Lord, I resign it.
> My dear Mother, for Christ's Sake be Comforted. Rejoyce in the Lord, for his mercies are infinite, and my Hope is, for the Merits of my Precious Saviour, to obtain Mercy.
> Ann Duck
> November 3, 1744
> From my Cell

Source: *The Ordinary of Newgate's, His Account of the Behaviour, Confession, and Dying Words of the Malefactors Who were Executed at Tyburn, 1703–72.*
See further: K. Chater, 'Hidden Histories: Black People in England During the British Slave Trade, 1600–1807' (PhD thesis, University of London, forthcoming).

Samuel Ajayi Crowther was the first black bishop in the Anglican church. He was appointed to a large and vaguely determined diocese in West Africa in 1864. In this photograph, taken in 1873, he and fellow black and white missionaries are seated beneath the Wilberforce Oak at Keston, Kent.

SAMUEL AJAYI CROWTHER c. 1809–91: Twice redeemed

Samuel Ajayi Crowther, born in southern Nigeria, was enslaved as a child and sold to a Portuguese trader whose ship was captured by a British warship on anti-slavery patrol. Along with other freed slaves and recaptives, he was landed at Freetown, Sierra Leone, in 1822. In this account, first published in 1837, Crowther describes the beginning of his formal education, and his desire to become a follower of Jesus Christ. Crowther went on to have a distinguished life. He wrote accounts of his journeys up the River Niger in 1841–42 and again in 1856; he studied West African languages and produced translations of the Bible; he was a missionary, was ordained as a minister in the Anglican Church, and became its first African bishop in 1864. Crowther first visited Britain in 1826, studied in London in 1842–43, and made several visits when he was a bishop. He received an honorary doctorate from Oxford University in 1864.

Letter of Mr. Samuel Crowther to the Rev. Wm. Jowett, in 1837, then
Secretary to the Church Missionary Society, Detailing the Circumstances
Connected with His Being Sold as s Slave.

... About six months after my arrival at Sierra Leone, I was able to read
the New Testament with some degree of freedom; and was made a
Monitor for which I was rewarded with sevenpence-halfpenny per month.
The Lord was pleased to open my heart to hearken to those things which
were spoken by His servants; and being convinced that I was a sinner,
and desired to obtain pardon through Jesus Christ, I was baptized on the
11th of December 1825, by the Rev. J. Raban ... May I ever have a fresh
desire to be engaged in the service of Christ, for it is *perfect freedom*!

Source: *Church Missionary Record*, 8 (October 1837), later reprinted as
Appendix III in the *Journals of Rev. James Frederick Schön and Mr. Samuel
Crowther* (London, 1842), pp. 371–385. A more recent source is in Philip
Curtin, ed., *Africa Remembered: Narratives by West Africans from the Era of the
Slave Trade* (Madison, 1968), ch. 9.

SAMUEL BARBER c. 1785–1828: A spiritual diary

Samuel Barber was the son of Francis Barber, the black servant of
Dr Samuel Johnson,[7] after whom he was named. Francis married a
white English woman, and Samuel, one of four children, was born
in London. The family moved to Staffordshire and Samuel was sent
to a boarding school in Lichfield. At the age of fourteen he became
a servant to a surgeon in Burslem. Samuel was converted at a
Methodist meeting in that town in 1805 or 1806, and he began to
teach in the Sunday school and to evangelize in the local workhouse.
His brief 'spiritual' diary of 1808 or 1809 has not survived, but it was
used when his obituary was written in 1829, from which this extract
is taken. Samuel moved to Tunstall, married Fanny Sherwin, and
became a Primitive Methodist local preacher. (See also p. 110.)

27th Aug: I find myself to be very barren, with respect to feeling a sense
of God's presence; though, bless his name, my desire is unto the
remembrance of him. I want to love and serve him with all my powers.
How long, O Lord, shall I be an outer-court worshipper? Oh quicken
me according to thy word.

28th: Still lingering in the way. Oh how the children of the world exceed me in diligence, after the things that perish! Quicken me, O God.

30th: How fast I am moving down the stream of time, and how little treasure laying up in heaven. Another day is gone; what have I been doing? Oh how little for my God! I want more power to stay my mind on heavenly things. I want a greater knowledge of my Saviour. I want to love him more. I want to behold more of the glory of God, shining in the face of Jesus Christ. Yet I would, I would be grateful for a little access to the throne of grace. Praise him from whom all blessings flow.

Source: John Smith, 'Memoir of Samuel Barber, a local preacher', *The Primitive Methodist Magazine for the Year 1829*, 10, pp. 88–89.

JAMES NEWBY c. 1840s–?: My conversion

James Newby, according to his story written in autobiographical form in the 1880s, was 'a prodigal' who 'in the far country ... came to himself'. He was born in the United States, the child of freed slaves. As a seaman he travelled over a large part of the world, arriving in Britain in the late 1860s or early 1870s. Newby was converted in 1873 while living in Scotland. Almost immediately he began to give his testimony at public meetings and within a year he had become an evangelist with a tent mission travelling in the Scottish midlands. Newby then trained in London and went to West Africa as a missionary. Ill health sent him home in 1879. He married in Britain and with his white wife returned to West Africa, this time to Liberia. There his wife died and Newby came home broken in health. James Newby was in Glasgow in 1884, but nothing is known of him thereafter.

Next Sunday I went back to the Mission Hall. Mr. Meek preached from John iii.16, but I was not in the slightest degree impressed by his discourse. After the first meeting was over I remained to the second one for what reason I do not know, as there was not the shadow of anxiety on my mind. But a Hand was leading me which I knew not, and leading me straight to the point where the arrow which He had in readiness could reach my soul, and bring me down to His feet, a willing captive ... The one question burning in my soul was, 'What if you should die to-night?'

And if I did, I saw that there was nothing but hell for me. Thus moved by fear – the very lowest of all motives – I was being prepared to receive the salvation of God...

Unable to rest, I ... walked through the streets ... my mind was so full of Scripture that it seemed as if I could read from the page of my memory as readily and clearly as from a book, so I began to repeat passages of Scripture ... On and on I went, but nothing I repeated had the desired effect or seemed to suit me at all, until I came to Luke xviii.13, 'God be merciful to me, a sinner!' At these words my soul seemed to stand still, for all at once I felt what it was to be a sinner, and then 'I groaned the sinner's only plea, God be merciful to me'...

'Jesus,' said I ... 'if Thou wilt keep me and not let me fall before all these temptations and evil habits, I will stick to Thee all the days of my life' ... Still I did not at that time experience full deliverance, but just a deep sense of relief, as if something had been settled ... I then pray[ed] ... in right earnest; and I did not leave off until I felt that I had completed my part of the transaction, and given myself unreservedly to Christ. Rising from my knees, I came out and stood right at the arch door; and well do I remember the surging feelings that rose within me as I stood there and felt myself to be indeed 'A slave redeemed from death and sin, A brand plucked from eternal fire.'[8]

Source: Elizabeth McHardie and Andrew Allan, *The Prodigal Continent or Her Prodigal Son and Missionary; or, the Adventures, Conversion and African Labours of Rev. James Newby* (London, 1885), 'My conversion', pp. 76–79.

SALIM WILSON c. 1860s–1946: Seeing the light

Salim Wilson, or Hatashil-Masha-Kathish, was a Dinka born in what is now the Sudan. Salim's father was killed while trying to protect his young child from capture by slave raiders. After several years as a slave Salim gained his freedom following a war. In 1879 he was employed as a servant by C. T. Wilson, a missionary working in the Sudan. Wilson brought Salim to England and he lived with the Wilson family in Nottingham. It was there, in the early 1880s, that Salim became a Christian and adopted the name of Wilson. (See also p. 67.)

The City of Nottingham will always seem one of the most important cities in the world to me, because it was there that I first actually saw the

Light, and at last came to know as Friend and Father the God who had been so beneficent to me in my tribulation when He was quite unknown to me.

Conversion did not come to me, as it has to so many, as a sudden flood, but rather as a gradual soaking in of the healing waters of Truth – not as a sudden blaze of light, but rather with the slow rising into radiance of the gentle English sun at dawn.

In Nottingham I found many kind friends. A large proportion of these were Christian ladies who were kind enough to take a deep interest in my welfare and to teach me hymns and how to read the Bible.

I progressed splendidly with the hymns, and was soon word-perfect in 'Jesus is my Shepherd' and 'Just as I am, without one Plea!' which I could thunder out with the best of them! With my Bible-reading I advanced fairly well, but much that I read I could not understand. Like my countrymen, mentioned in the Acts,[9] I needed the teaching of God's Holy Spirit.

I had many good friends to help me in my difficulties, and they prayed for me continually. Every day prayers for my enlightenment and conversion rose up to God, and gradually, and in His own good time, these prayers were answered. I reached the stage when I could sincerely pray for myself, that Light might be vouchsafed to me.

It came at last, on an occasion when I read the Gospel of St. John, iii, 16–18, and found there a message for me. I read and re-read, and presently I was at last able to see God's way of salvation clearly. I was able to draw a comparison from my own stormy life:

My dear Father had died for me. He could have saved himself, but he chose to die rather than desert his son. In his grand effort to save me from destruction he braved a terrible death and perished before my eyes.

Now I could see that in just the same way had Christ chosen to die for me and for the whole world of sinners – that we might be saved from eternal destruction. My father had died to save me from the bondage of my body – Christ had died to save me from the bondage of sin.

Source: Salim Wilson, *I Was a Slave* (London, n.d., c. 1939), pp. 228–229.

G. DANIELS EKARTE c. 1890s–1964: My conversion

Daniels Ekarte came from Calabar in southern Nigeria. As a boy he came into contact with Mary Slessor (1848–1915), the pioneer

Pastor Daniels Ekarte lived in Liverpool for most of his life, where he ran the African Churches Mission. This photograph and text come from a 1937 issue of *The Keys*, the journal of the League of Coloured Peoples.

Scottish missionary who worked among the Okoyong people. Unlike many white missionaries, Slessor's life was an example of African inculturation – she lived in African style as head of a household of woman and children. Although there is no documentary evidence of Ekarte's relationship with Slessor, clearly from his own account she had a great impact on the young man. At some time Ekarte became a seaman and arrived in Liverpool, probably in 1915. Here he describes his 'reconversion' in 1922. In 1931 he opened the African Churches Mission in Liverpool, which he served as pastor for over thirty years. (See also p. 135.)

MY CONVERSION

[Arriving at Liverpool] ... I was welcomed not by the saints of England, but by bitter disappointments. From the very moment of my landing ... I was reminded that I was a dreamer ... I became victim of circumstances, I was tempted and ... I became a partner of some vicious occupations, I came in contact with men of different nationality and mentality, to whom salvation of soul was unknown ...

Although for years I was separated from the life of a 'holy man,' yet still I could always feel the presence of God in all I did. Though forced to live the life of a debarred man, I was not altogether without hope of salvation. I had no pleasure in all I was doing. The life I was living was an abomination to me, but who will re-kindle faith in me ... one day I took a walk down the dock, I saw some coloured men worshipping in a room, I went in, but was not impressed.

I went on another occasion, and on that occasion my faith was restored to me; I was re-converted, saved and pardoned. The lines came to my mind, 'When thou art strong, strengthen thy brother.'[10]

Gold and silver have I none, but use me, O Lord, to devote my life for the salvation of my brethren in Liverpool, for their spiritual welfare and the knowledge of Thy Word. To this end I have dedicated my life, for this cause shall I work until I see thee face to face. These words are my daily prayer.

Source: Daniels Ekarte, 'My conversion', African Churches Mission pamphlet, Rhodes House Library, Oxford. Anti-Slavery Society Papers, Br. Emp. Mss. S.23, Box H 1/2 1.
See further: Marika Sherwood, *Pastor Daniels Ekarte and the African Churches Mission* (London, 1994).

Notes

1. Jonathan Edwards, 1703–58, Congregational pastor and Calvinist theologian in Massachusetts. His preaching contributed to the first 'Great Awakening' in the British North American colonies.
2. George Whitefield, 1714–70, Anglican clergyman and evangelist whose many preaching visits to North America contributed to the 'Great Awakening'. He accepted slavery and owned slaves.
3. Richard Baxter, 1615–91, Puritan pastor, leader, and prolific author. His *A Call to the Unconverted* (1657) became a major evangelistic book.
4. William Murray, 1st Earl of Mansfield, 1705–93, judge and politician, who sat on the King's Bench from 1756.
5. Charles Wesley, 1707–88, Methodist leader and brother of John Wesley.
6. John Wesley, 1703–91, the founder of Methodism.
7. Samuel Johnson (1700–84), compiler of an English dictionary first published in 1755.

8. A variation of Amos 4:11.

9. He is referring to the Ethiopian diplomat and his entourage mentioned in Acts 8:26–39.

10. A variation of Luke 22:32.

2. PREACHING

PHILIP QUAQUE 1741–1816:
Missionary priest on the Gold Coast

Quaque, from the Gold Coast (modern Ghana), was sponsored by the Society for the Propagation of the Gospel in Foreign Parts (SPG)[1] for education in England with the idea that he should return to West Africa as a missionary. Quaque spent ten years in England. He was ordained as a priest in the Church of England and, with his white English wife, returned home in 1766 as 'Missionary, School Master, and Catechist to the Negroes on the Gold Coast'. Quaque also served as 'Chaplain' to the small handful of Europeans employed by the Company of Merchants Trading to Africa.

Cape Coast Castle
Africa
March 7th, 1767
The morning after New Year's Day, I took my first visit to Anomabu where I lodged in the house of one Richard Brew, Esq., an English merchant, by the kind recommendation of Samuel Smith, Esq. (his bosom friend) who was then a member of the Committee [of the

Company of Merchants] and aboded with him for the space of a week,
during which time he behaved in the most polite manner imaginable.
And on the Sunday read prayers and preached in his most noble hall
to a very good audience. The divine service being ended, I immediately
reported to the table where I had already fixed my element for
christening and did then and there lawfully baptise his two mulatto
daughters, by his own earnest desire, and three others besides, to
the universal satisfaction of the whole congregation both white and
black then assembled, and gave certificates before I took my farewell
of him.

Source: Rhodes House Library, Oxford. Papers of the Society for the
Propagation of the Gospel in Foreign Parts.
See further: Margaret Priestley, 'Philip Quaque of the Cape Coast' in
Philip D. Curtin, *Africa Remembered: Narratives by West Africans from the Era
of the Slave Trade* (Madison, WI, 1968), ch. 3; Paul Edwards and David
Dabydeen, eds., *Black Writers in Britain 1760–1890* (Edinburgh, 1991),
pp. 101–116.

JUPITER HAMMON 1711–c. 1800:
Salvation by Christ alone

Throughout his life Jupiter Hammon was a slave to the Lloyd
family, prosperous merchants who lived on Long Island, New York.
Hammon (not related to Briton Hammon) was a lay preacher. He
had several poems published, including one addressed to the black
poet Phillis Wheatley, some sermons, and *An Address to the Negroes in
the State of New York* (1779), in which he urged slaves to bear their
condition with patience while striving to persuade their masters
to free their children. The Lloyds were loyal to the British cause
and at the start of the Revolutionary War they fled to Hartford,
Connecticut, taking Hammon with them. 'Evening thought', from
which this extract is taken, is among the earliest known pieces of
writing by an African American.

AN EVENING THOUGHT. SALVATION BY CHRIST, WITH
PENITENTIAL CRIES:
Composed by Jupiter Hammon, a Negro Belonging to Mr. Lloyd, of
Queen's-Village, on Long-Island, the 25th of December, 1760.

SALVATION comes by Jesus Christ alone,
  The only Son of God;
Redemption now to every one,
  That love his holy Word.
Dear Jesus we would fly to Thee,
  And leave off every Sin,
Thy tender Mercy well agree;
  Salvation from our King.
Salvation comes now from the Lord,
  Our victorious King;
His holy Name be well ador'd,
  Salvation surely bring.
Dear Jesus give thy Spirit now,
  Thy Grace to every Nation,
That han't [have not] the Lord to whom we bow,
  The Author of Salvation.

Source: Oscar Wegelin, *Jupiter Hammon, American Negro Poet* (New York, 1915), pp. 29–31.
See further: Vincent Carretta, *Unchained Voices: An Anthology of Black Authors in the English-Speaking World of the 18th Century* (Lexington, 1996), pp. 26–28.

PHILLIS WHEATLEY: On the death of George Whitefield

Phillis Wheatley's poem on the death of the evangelist George Whitefield[2] attracted the attention of people in Britain. Phillis met the great preacher at the Wheatleys' home shortly before his death. Among Whitefield's principal supporters in Britain was Selena Hastings, Countess of Huntingdon.[3] Phillis addressed her poem on Whitefield's death to the Countess, and as a result she became widely known in England, a country she visited briefly in mid 1773. On her return to America, Phillis was given her freedom; she married and had several children. (See also pp. 57, 74.)

On the Death of the Rev. Mr. GEORGE WHITEFIELD. 1770.

Behold the prophet in his tow'ring flight!
He leaves the earth for heav'n's unmeasur'd height,
And worlds unknown receive him from our sight.

There *Whitefield* wings with rapid course his way,
And sails to *Zion* through vast seas of day.
Thy pray'rs, great saint, and thine incessant cries
Have pierc'd the bosom of thy native skies.
Thou moon hast seen, and all the stars of light,
How he has wrestled with his God by night.
He pray'd that grace in ev'ry heart might dwell,
He long'd to see *America* excel;
He charg'd its youth that ev'ry grace divine
Should with full lustre in their conduct shine;
That Saviour, which his soul did first receive,
The greatest gift that ev'n a God can give,
He freely offer'd to the num'rous throng,
That on his lips with list'ning pleasure hung.

'Take him, ye wretched, for your only good,
Take him ye starving sinners, for your food;
Ye thirsty, come to this life-giving stream,
Ye preachers, take him for your joyful theme;
Take him my dear *Americans*, he said,
Be your complaints on his kind bosom laid:
Take him, ye *Africans*, he longs for you,
Impartial Saviour is his title due:
Wash'd in the fountain of redeeming blood,
You shall be sons, and kings, and priests to God'...

Source: *Phillis Wheatley: Poems on Various Subjects, Religious and Moral*
(London, 1773), pp. 22–24.
See further: *Phillis Wheatley: Complete Writings*, ed. Vincent Carretta
(London, 2001).

JOHN JEA 1773–18?: Preaching in the British Isles

John Jea was born in Old Calabar, on the Atlantic coast of what is
now Nigeria. At the age of two he was kidnapped and enslaved and
sold to America. By the time he was fifteen years old, Jea had taught
himself to read and had become a Christian. He gained his freedom
and became a roving preacher and also a seaman, serving on ships
that crossed the Atlantic to Ireland and England. Jea was a

Methodist and a pacifist, and his long experience of slavery and racial discrimination also made him politically radical. But above all he was an evangelical who described his conversion as a time 'when my heart was changed by divine grace, and I became regenerated and born again of the water and of the Spirit, and became as a little child'. In Ireland, where Jea married an Irish wife, probably in the 1790s, he continued his preaching 'from Limerick to Cork'.

> I preached in Limerick and the country villages round, and by the Spirit of God, many people were convinced and converted. I also preached to the regiment, at the request of the commanding officer and the mayor of Limerick. The mayor was so kind as to go with me to protect me from the Romans [Roman Catholics]; for they were much inveterated against me, and said they would have my life. And when the mayor did not go with me, a guard of soldiers was sent. By the command of the mayor and the commanding officer, five of the Roman priests were brought before them, and ordered to give a reason why they were so malicious against me. They could only say, that I would not believe their doctrine, neither would they believe mine; and one of the head priests said, that I was going to hell. Then three of the priests said unto them, 'We cannot deny or dispute his doctrine.' Then they went out full of rage and fury, and determined to lay in wait for my life ... Thus I spoke in the name of Jesus.

Jea was captured by a French ship and spent five years in captivity in France, where he learned French. He refused to fight against the British and eventually he made his way to Britain via Guernsey, in the Channel Islands. Jea settled near Portsmouth, where he continued to preach. His life story, in which he described himself as 'The African Preacher', was published in 1815. Nothing is known of Jea after 1817.

> I arrived safely at Guernsey, and brotherly love did not withdraw itself from me there, for the brethren in Christ gladly received me, and gave me the right-hand of fellowship, treated me as a brother, and gave me liberty to preach in the different chapels; and I can say with truth, there was no chapel large enough to hold the congregations. I remained there fifteen days, and during that time there were many souls convinced and converted to God. After that I departed ... for Southampton ... and

thank God, I arrived there in safety, and was cordially received by the brethren, who gave me the use of their chapels to preach in, and much good was done during my stay … Now, dear reader, I trust by the grace of God, that the small house in Hawk Street [Portsea], which the Lord hath been pleased to open unto me, for the public worship of his great and glorious name, will be filled with converts, and that my feeble labours will be crowned with abundant success.

Source: John Jea, *The Life, History and Unparalleled Sufferings of John Jea, The African Preacher. Compiled and Written by Himself* (Portsea, c. 1815), pp. 82–83, 94–95.
See further: Graham Russell Hodges, ed., *Black Itinerants of the Gospel: The Narratives of John Jea and George White* (New York, 1993; New York, 2002).

In 1816 John Jea had published *A Collection of Hymns*, twenty-nine of which appear to be written by him as they contain references to his own experiences of slavery and freedom; others were by Isaac Watts[4] and Charles Wesley.[5]

Works of Creation

AFRICA nations, great and small,
   Upon this earthly ball,
Give glory to the God above,
   And crown him Lord of all.

By God's free grace they run the race,
   And did his glory see,
To preach the gospel to our race,
   The gospel liberty.

Trusting in Christ

I thank God, that did set
   My soul at liberty;
My body freed from men below,
   By his almighty grace.

I will be slave no more,
   Since Christ has set me free,
He nail'd my tyrants to the cross,
   And bought me liberty.

Source: John Jea, *A Collection of Hymns. Compiled and Selected by John Jea,
African Preacher of the Gospel* (Portsea, 1816).
See further: Hodges, *Black Itinerants of the Gospel*, pp. 165–177.

SIMEON WILHELM c. 1800–17:
A pious young man's appeal

Simeon Wilhelm was born in the Rio Pongas region of West Africa.
He was a devout young man and attended a Church Missionary
Society (CMS)[6] school. In 1816 he agreed to accompany the CMS
missionary Edward Bickersteth to Britain so that he could be
trained and then return as a missionary to his own people. While
attending the National School in Shoe Lane, London, Simeon fell ill
and died on 29 August 1817. He was buried in St Bride's, Fleet
Street. Simeon Wilhelm's piety and Christian faith greatly impressed
Bickersteth and others. Bickersteth used extracts from two letters
that Simeon wrote, and he also quoted, although not verbatim,
words that the African boy spoke on his deathbed. The language is
pious and heavily sentimental but common to evangelical Christian
literature of the period.

> O! what a good thing it is for Christians to have God for their Father,
> and to be joint-heirs with Jesus Christ! Everlasting life! O that happy life
> for Christians where they shall praise their God; and be in heaven with
> him. Worldly men! See how sweet it is to be happy with God and try
> now to pray to God, THIS DAY, while he is near and may be found ...
> To be born again is to get a new heart, to have our corrupt nature
> changed, to lead a new life ... The mere professions of religion are the
> worst part of mankind, and will have a double portion of punishment.
> If you would be a Christian, be not only a professor, but get a new heart,
> and thirst after righteousness.

Shortly before Simeon's last illness, he wrote several letters to
different friends.

Church Missionary House,

June 10, 1817

I should like to inform you the news which I heard from Africa; that
churches were building among my own nation; and some of them
profess that they will be Christians, and be baptized. It is certainly true,
that the Ethiopians are beginning to stretch out their hands to God,[7]
their Heavenly Father. Oh, let the time come soon, when all the ends of
the earth shall worship the Lord their God, and all the nations call Him
blessed! when Europe and Africa shall join to celebrate, in different
tongues, the love of the Saviour!

Church Missionary House

June 28, 1817

Remember Simeon in your prayers, that he may be useful to his
Countrymen, who lie *in darkness and in the shadow of Death. They do not know
their Saviour who died for them.* Oh pray for poor Africa, that the Society's
labours be not in vain! I do not forget your kindness to me, when you
was in London. I pray for you. I hope the Lord will answer my prayer.
He is a God that heareth prayer. If I only ask right things of Him, He
will give them me.

On 1 August, Bickersteth wrote of Simeon that, 'after having prayed
with him, he prayed himself, as nearly as I can recollect, in the
following words':

O Lord, Maker of heaven and earth, Thou createdst all things and me.
Look down with thy compassion on me! O Lord Jesus, have compassion
on me! Pardon all my sins! I am a great sinner. Forgive me what I have
done amiss. Give me a deep sense of my sinfulness, and of Thy
pardoning grace; *that I may go to Africa, and preach to my poor benighted
Countrymen, the unsearchable riches of Christ!*

Source: Edward Bickersteth, *Memoirs of Simeon Wilhelm, A Native of the Susoo
Country, West Africa* (New Haven, 1819), pp. 27–29, 33.

ALEXANDER CRUMMELL 1819–98:
'Ethiopia shall soon stretch out her hands unto God'
Crummell was a born a freeman in New York City and ordained in

the Episcopalian Church. In 1847 he came to England and from 1851 to 1853 he studied at Queens' College, Cambridge University. He lived in Ipswich and became curate of St Stephen's Church. Crummell left Britain to live and work in Liberia, a republic recently established in West Africa as a place of liberty for African Americans. In this sermon, given to the Ladies Negro Education Society at Hotwell's Church, Clifton, Bristol, on 21 April 1852, he used as his text Psalm 68:31, 'Ethiopia shall soon stretch out her hands unto Africa.' This text was often used by black preachers to encourage other black people to join in missionary work to win Ethiopia – the term often used in the Bible to refer to the whole of Africa – for Christ. After twenty years' work in Liberia and Sierra Leone, Crummell returned to the United States to take charge of St Mary's Mission in Washington, DC.

I cannot but believe that the day of Africa's redemption fast draweth nigh! And vast and extensive as the work may be, it seems that it will be a most rapid one ... I have the strongest impression of the nigh approach of her bright day of deliverance. The night, I am convinced – the night of forlornness, of agony and desolation – is far spent; the day is at hand! The black charter of crime and infamy and blood, which for nigh three centuries has given up my fatherland to the spoiler, is about to be erased ... And if I read the signs of the time aright ... I see God's hand graciously opened for Africa ... what a grand reversal of a dark destiny will it not be for poor bleeding Africa! What a delightful episode from the hopeless agony of her unmitigated, unalleviated suffering! For ages hath she lain beneath the incubus of the 'demon of her idolatry.' For ages hath she suffered the ravages of vice, corruption, iniquity, and guilt. For ages hath she been 'stricken, and smitten' by the deadly thrusts of murder and hate, revenge and slaughter. Fire, famine, and the sword have been her distressful ravaging visitations. War, with devastating stride, has ravaged her fair fields, and peopled her open and voracious tombs. The slave trade – that fell destroyer! – has sacked her cities, has turned the hands of her sons upon each other, and set her different communities at murderous strife, and colored their hands with fraternal blood! ... Earth has had her beauty marred by the bloody track of the cruel men who have robbed my fatherland of her children ... But now there is a new spirit abroad – not only in the Christian world, but likewise through the different quarters of her own broad continent. There is an uprising of her sons from intellectual sloth and spiritual inertness; a seeking and a stretching forth of her hands, for light, instruction, and spirituality, such as the world has never before seen; and which gives hopes that the days of Cyprian and Augustine shall again return to Africa; when the giant sins and the deadly evils which have ruined her, shall be effectively stayed; and when Ethiopia … 'shall stretch out her hands unto God!'

Source: Alexander Crummell, *The Future of Africa* (New York, 1862).

THOMAS L. JOHNSON 1836–1921: My first sermon

Thomas L. Johnson was born in Virginia as a slave and he remained so until 1865. He became a Christian and a Baptist preacher. Johnson's aim was to be a missionary to Africa but he was also conscious of his lack of education. In 1876 he came to Britain and entered The Pastor's College in London.[8] As a student training for the Baptist ministry, he was required to practise preaching. His first sermon was given to a class of critical fellow students at the College. (See also pp. 113–114, 118.)

My anxiety as to my first sermon in College was very great, as any student may imagine, for I had heard other sermons criticised. I preached from Acts xvi. 31. I studied up the subject night and day. Before coming from America I had been presented with three volumes of Andrew Fuller's works.[9] I read these works diligently, and was struck with his remarks – that to be born again was to be 're-created' – and I found some passages that just suited my subject. Notwithstanding that I was told not to 'plagiarise,' I felt that I could not say the thing better myself, and so made use of some expressions which I found answered the subject. I thought that the book, being old, no-one would detect it; the students would be sure to be taken up with the new books. But the students went for me when I had finished my sermon. However, when they had done with me, Professor Rogers, who presided, said: 'I don't think our brother is deserving of such severe criticism. (Hear, Hear). If Mr. Johnson, who is forty years old, and having no advantages, can study the English Grammar – (Hear, Hear) – it shows what he is capable of. Look at him, brethren, I see in him an

Thomas L. Johnson, a former American slave, was a Baptist minister and missionary, and always an evangelist. He settled in Britain and spoke at meetings all over the country. He often illustrated his talks with slave chains and a whip, to demonstrate that all people are slaves to sin and can only be rescued by Christ's redeeming love.

"Andrew Fuller!"' The students cheered and clapped and thumped the desks, and one brother shouted, 'Cheer up, Johnson.' Thus ended the first sermon.

Source: Thomas L. Johnson, *Twenty-Eight Years a Slave or the Story of My Life in Three Continents* (Bournemouth, 7th edn, 1909), p. 94.

AMANDA SMITH 1837–1915: A woman preacher

Amanda Smith was born of slave parents in Maryland, USA. She was converted in 1856. Her first husband disappeared during the civil war; her second died. Thereafter Amanda travelled as a holiness preacher speaking at camp meetings and in churches. In 1878 she began an overseas ministry, visiting Britain where she preached in many churches and spoke at an after-meeting of the Keswick

Convention. From 1879 to 1890 Amanda was a missionary in India and then in Liberia. From 1899 to her death, she ran a children's orphanage in Illinois. In 1879 she spoke at a Presbyterian meeting in Scotland although there were many people there who disapproved of a woman preaching.

> Of course, I was a curiosity to start with. The hall was crowded. The first two meetings they were afraid what I was going to do. But I was judicious and careful, and the Lord helped me wonderfully. By the time I got through, no one could have told from their manner, but what they had been accustomed not only to women preaching, but to black women all their days.

Source: Amanda Smith, *Autobiography* (Chicago, 1893).

J. ALBERT THORNE 1860–1939: Practical encouragement

Albert Thorne came from Barbados to Britain in 1884. He gave lectures around the country while he studied to gain admission to university in order to study medicine. On his first visit to London he attended a service in a mission that had as patrons the well-known evangelicals Lord and Lady Kinnaird.[10] The mission organizers were clearly impressed with Thorne and mentioned his name to the Kinnairds.

> About two or three days after, I received a very kind letter from her Ladyship, stating that it had afforded her much pleasure to hear of me ... and that Lord Kinnaird and herself should be pleased if I would come and spend a day or two with them (at their country seat in Kent). I went down ... and was received as a prince among princes and it touched me to see those ladies in high position, going 'in the streets and highways and compelling them to come in', in order that the Father's house might be filled.

Source: 'Tackling a great problem I', *Jamaica Times*, 15 January 1910.
See further: Robert A. Hill, 'Zion on the Zambezi: Dr J. Albert Thorne, "A descendant of Africa of Barbados", and the African colonial enterprise: The "preliminary stage", 1894–7', in Jagdish S. Gundara and Ian Duffield, eds., *Essays on the History of Blacks in Britain* (Aldershot, 1992), p. 102.

SALIM WILSON c. 1860s–1946: Public speaking

Salim Wilson, a freed slave from the Sudan, became a Christian in
1882. An idea common in certain missionary societies was that
Africans should be trained in Britain and then return as missionaries to their own countries. Salim shared this idea and was sent
to Cliff College, the Methodist training institution in Derbyshire
in 1882–83 and again in 1884–86. Part of his training involved
speaking at churches and public meetings. Here is his description
of going to speak at Burton-on-Trent with two Africans from the
Congo. (See also p. 119.)

I had my first taste of public speaking. My young friends from the Congo
and myself were taken to Burton-on-Trent (where, by the way, I saw
more beer barrels than I had ever imagined existed in the world!), and we
attended a number of meetings, at most of which were present seven or
eight hundred people.

I felt dreadfully nervous when called upon to say a few words to what
seemed to me in those days a vast audience, but I managed to survive the
ordeal quite well, and felt very pleased with myself afterwards that I had
not broken down.

We stayed that night with the vicar of Trinity Church, and it was quite
a happy and lively party that gathered round his hospitable supper-table
that evening. It was a charming and peaceful scene, but, curiously enough,
two of those present were destined to meet in the future amid very
different surroundings – for, some five year later, I and one of the other
guests met unexpectedly in the savage wilderness of the distant Congo.

Source: Salim Wilson, *I Was a Slave* (London, n.d., c. 1939), pp. 229–230.

PETER STANFORD 1859–1909:
A black Baptist pastor, Birmingham

Peter Stanford was born a slave in Virginia in 1859. He was parted
from his parents during the Civil War, lived with Native Americans,
who also abandoned him, but was then found by members of the
Society of Friends, who placed him in an orphanage in Boston.
From there Stanford was 'adopted' by a man named Stanford who
used him as unpaid labour. Peter ran away and lived a wild life. In
1874 he was converted at a meeting where the American preacher,

D. L. Moody,[11] was speaking. Stanford became a Baptist minister and moved to Canada. He came to Britain in 1883 to raise money for his struggling church. He moved to Birmingham, married, and then in 1889 accepted the call to become minister of a local Baptist church. Stanford took great pride in this, as is clear from this brief chapter in his autobiography, written when he was twenty-nine years old; but his appointment was not without difficulties. In 1895 Stanford left Hope Street and returned to the United States.

I AM PASTOR OF AN ENGLISH BAPTIST CHURCH, WITH MY GOOD NAME VINDICATED BEFORE THE WORLD.

On May 5th, 1889, I received and accepted the following Call from the Baptist Church, Hope Street, Birmingham:

Baptist Church,
Hope Street,
Birmingham,
May 8th, 1889.

To the Rev. P. T. Stanford.

Revd. and Dear Sir,
At a meeting on Wednesday, May the 6th, it was unanimously decided that we, the members and congregation attending the above place of worship, invite you to become our Pastor. You know our condition will not allow us to offer you a large salary, but we offer you our prayers, willing hearts, and hands. Remember, dear Brother, this call is from God, and He has promised to supply all our needs. Trusting you will see your way to accept our offer.
We are, yours faithfully,
Signed on behalf of the Church,
D. BAILEY.
H. SMITH.
T. BARBER.
J. MADDOCKS.
H. GREENHILL.
HENRY RICHARDS.
JAS. CLARK, Secretary.

I was not allowed to take my position however until after a stern fight in which, through the grace of God and the kindness of the Rev. Chas. Joseph,[12] and my solicitor, A. P. Carr, Esq, of Birmingham, I at last came off more than conquerer. And to-day, notwithstanding my birth as a slave and the colour of my skin, I am pastor in this great city of Birmingham. I have been libelled, slandered, ostracised, suspected, and opposed; but in all these troubles I have not lacked many true christian friends whose names my gratitude prompts me to print here, only I know too well that any public mention of their virtues or their deeds of love would but offend their finer susceptibilities. I therefore forbear, and giving thanks to God, bid adieu to my readers.

Source: Peter Thomas Stanford, *From Bondage to Liberty: Being the life story of the Rev. P. T. Stanford who was once a slave! And is now the recognised pastor of an English Baptist church* (Smethwick, 1889), ch. XIV.
See further: Paul Walker, 'The Revd Peter Thomas Stanford (1860–1909) Birmingham's "Coloured Preacher" ' (unpublished PhD thesis, Manchester University), 2004.

TANIMOWO T. SOLARY, 1942: A tribute to 'one of Africa's greatest sons', James Emman Kwegyir Aggrey

James Edward Kwegyir Aggrey (1875–1927) was born in the British West African colony of the Gold Coast (modern Ghana). He studied at Livingstone College, and then at Columbia University in New York. Aggrey was a gentle, scholarly teacher, greatly respected by most people who met him. He was appointed as the only African member of the two Commissions sent by the Phelps-Stokes Fund[13] to look at and report on educational provision in Africa in 1920–21 and in 1922–24. Aggrey was appointed Assistant Vice-Principal of the Prince of Wales' College, Achimota (the 'Eton of West Africa') in 1925. He died in New York. This Address, by the Revd. Tanimowo T. Solary, was given at an Aggrey tombstone memorial held by the West African Students' Union[14] in November 1942. (See also p. 131.)

We are met here to pay tribute to the memory of one of Africa's greatest sons ... he was a true soldier equipped with weapons that disarmed his staunchest opponents, a great protagonist for all that promote

understanding and goodwill between man and man, an apostle of
reconciliation and inter-racial co-operation. Aggrey was essentially a man
of peace ... the world will continue to remember him by his Parable of
The Black and the White Keys of the Piano ... 'Intelligent co-operation,
mutual respect and racial interdependence'; a realisation that each of the
peoples of the world have their own contribution to make which no
other can, and that each would be poorer without the co-operation
of the other.

Harmony from the Black and the White keys means that each key,
whether white or black, must be the best key possible in order to be
able to fulfil its function. That was why Aggrey devoted his life to the
uplift of Africa, and advocated and supported educational schemes,
health programmes and everything that would be of help to improve,
preserve and develop the cultural heritage of Africans ... Aggrey ...
had unbounded faith in the capacity of Africans to rise to great
things ...

Aggrey, if he were here, would be the first to acknowledge that his
life was fed from the secret springs of God ... You who would honour
Aggrey's memory, who would emulate his virtues who work and plan
for Aggrey's Africa, you cannot afford to ignore Aggrey's God. Aggrey
was first and foremost a Christian ... Whoever may be false, Aggrey's
Saviour and Lord remains true, and is willing and able to lead us to the
desired goal. For it is His world and no plans can succeed from which
God is banished. Aggrey is dead, but his soul keeps marching on. Aggrey
is gone but Aggrey's God remains. Would to God that Elijah's mantle
shall fall upon some Elisha this day.

Source: The League of Coloured Peoples *News Letter* 41 (February 1943),
pp. 141–144.
See further: Edwin A. Smith, *Aggrey of Africa: A Study in Black and White*
(London, 1929).

ANON: An encounter in a railway carriage 1940s

The League of Coloured Peoples (LCP), founded by Dr Harold
Moody in 1931, was a black-run organization but with a multiracial
membership. Moody regarded the LCP as a Christian body. The
League's regular journal *The Keys* and its wartime successor the *News
Letter* contained reports on efforts to combat racial discrimination

in Britain and in the British Empire, plus information about the achievements of black people. Moody liked to include brief stories that reflected well on the behaviour of black people when confronted with white ignorance and prejudice. This account was published at the height of the Second World War.

TRUE STORY SENT BY ONE OF OUR MEMBERS IN
HERTFORD

Two women got into a railway carriage, one corner of which was occupied by a black gentleman. 'Look at that poor heathen there! I don't suppose he even knows that he has a soul to save!' The 'poor heathen' overheard and leaning forward asked the good lady if she could tell him in what way he could obtain information as to the saving of his soul. Quite nonplussed she suggested that he should visit a minister of religion, mentioning that her own vicar was a very 'nice man.' 'But can you yourself not help in any way?' asked the 'poor heathen'. 'Have you nothing I could read – no book of any sort?' 'Well, of course there is the Bible; you could read that! But I haven't got one with me now.' 'But I have,' replied the 'poor heathen.' And taking from his pocket the New Testament, he proceeded to preach the 'true gospel' to every one in the carriage for the rest of the journey.

Source: The League of Coloured Peoples *News Letter* 44 (May 1943), p. 22.

Notes
1. The SPG, founded in 1701 by high Church of England clergy, directed all its attention on the colonies.
2. See above, p. 53, note 2.
3. Selina Hastings, Countess of Huntingdon (1707–91), Calvinist Methodist and evangelical leader.
4. Isaac Watts, 1674–1748, the father of English hymnody.
5. See above, p. 53, note 5.
6. The CMS, influenced by evangelicals of the Church of England, was founded in 1799.
7. A reference to Psalm 68:31, commonly used by black Christians from the late eighteenth century.

8. The Pastor's College, now Spurgeon's College, was founded by the great Baptist preacher Charles Haddon Spurgeon in 1856.
9. Andrew Fuller, 1754–1815, Baptist theologian and first secretary of the Baptist Missionary Society, founded in 1792.
10. Arthur (1814–87) and Mary (1816–88) Kinnaird were prominent Anglicans actively involved in many evangelical causes and interests.
11. Dwight L. Moody, 1837–99, US preacher, who, with Ira D. Sankey, conducted evangelical tours in Britain in 1873–5 and 1881–4.
12. Charles Joseph, minister who became president of the Baptist Union in 1914.
13. In her will of 1909, Caroline Phelps-Stokes gave her fortune to be used 'for the education of Negroes, both in Africa and the United States, North American Indians and needy and deserving white students'.
14. The West African Students' Union (WASU) was formed in London in 1925.

3. PROTEST AND POLITICS

BLACK TOM or DAVID SPENS:
Denouncing 'tyrannical power' 1770

Black slaves brought to Britain in the eighteenth century often falsely believed that baptism would give them their freedom. This was clearly believed by Black Tom, who probably came to Scotland in the 1760s, and who belonged to Dr Dalrymple. Tom ran away, took shelter with a farmer, and was baptized as David Spens in the parish church of East Wemyss in September 1769. Dr Dalrymple went to the Court of Sessions to try to get his slave – his property – returned to him. Four lawyers opposed this and drew up a deposition in Spens's name. Local miners and salters collected money to help Spens. Spens gained his freedom and returned to work for the farmer who had befriended him. The case is important because it was two years before Lord Mansfield's judgment in London which said that a slave in England and Wales could not be returned to the colonies. In Scotland, which had a separate legal system, the decision of *Wedderburn v. Knight* in 1778 was that 'the state of slavery is not recognised by the laws of this kingdom'. Here is part of Spens's deposition.

I David Spence formerly called Black Tom late Slave to Dr David
Dalrymple of Lindifferen Hereby intimate to you the said Dr Dalrymple
that being formerly an heathen Slave to you & of Consequence then at
your Sole disposal but being now instructed in the Christian Religion I
have embraced the same and been publickly Baptized to the ffaith (sic)
by the Reverend Mr Harry Spence Minr of the Gospel at Wemyss & so
admitted as member of the Church of Christ established in the Kingdom
and of Consequence I am now by the Christian Religion Liberate and set
at freedom from my old yoke bondage and Slavery and by the Laws of
this Christian land there is no Slavery nor vestige of Slavery allowed
nevertheless you take it upon you to exercise your old Tyrannical Power
over me and would dispose of me arbitrarily at your despotic will &
Pleasure and for that end you threaten to send me abroad out of this
Country to the West Indies and there dispose of me for money by which
you not only Subvert the Ends and designs of the Christian institution
which ransoms Liberty to all its members But also you would deprive our
Sovereign Lord the King of a good Subject

Source: Paul Edwards and James Walvin, *Black Personalities in the Era of the
Slave Trade* (London, 1983), pp. 160–161.

PHILLIS WHEATLEY: A 'cry for liberty'

Phillis Wheatley was given her freedom in October 1773 after her
return home to Boston from London. In this letter, written in
February 1774, to the Revd Samson Occom (1723–92), a Native
American Christian evangelist, Phillis denounces slavery. She also
hoped that the challenge to British rule in the North American colonies would lead to the end of slavery there. (See also pp. 41, 57, 109.)

Rev'd and honor'd Sir,
I have this Day received your obliging kind Epistle, and am greatly
satisfied with your Reasons respecting the Negroes, and think highly
reasonable what you offer in Vindication of their natural Rights: Those
that invade them cannot be insensible that the divine Light is chasing
away the thick Darkness which broods over the Land of Africa; and the
Chaos which has reign'd so long, is converting into beautiful Order, and
[r]eveals more and more clearly, the glorious Dispensation of civil and
religious Liberty, which are so inseparably united, that there is little or no

Enjoyment of one without the other: Otherwise, perhaps, the Israelites had been less solicitous for their Freedom from Egyptian Slavery; I do not say they would have been contented without it, by no means, for in every human Breast, God has implanted a Principle, which we call Love of Freedom; it is impatient of Oppression, and pants for Deliverance ... I will assert, that the same Principle lives in us. God grant Deliverance in his own Way and Time...

Printed in *Connecticut Gazette; and the Universal Intelligencer*, 11 March 1774.

Source: *Phillis Wheatley: Complete Writings*, ed. Vincent Carretta (London, 2001), pp. 152–153.

IGNATIUS SANCHO c. 1729–80:
The slave trade 'uniformly wicked' 1778

Ignatius Sancho was born on a slave ship in the Atlantic taking him to Spanish America. His parents died and Sancho's owner took the young orphan to Britain and gave him to three ladies in Greenwich. They thought to keep him ignorant, but fortunately the alert young man attracted the attention of the Duke of Montague, who lent him books and encouraged his education. Eventually Sancho became valet to the Montague family. He married a black lady in 1758, and opened a grocer's shop in Westminster in 1774. He knew the painter Thomas Gainsborough, who painted his portrait, and also Laurence Sterne the novelist, with whom he corresponded. Sancho's letters were published in 1782, two years after his death. Little is known about Sancho's Christian faith, but he condemned the slave trade on the West African coast, which he knew was a trade of mutual advantage both to white traders and also to African rulers. (See also p. 125.)

I say it is with reluctance, that I must observe your country's conduct has been uniformly wicked in the East – West Indies – and even on the coast of Guinea. The grand object of the English navigators – indeed of all Christian navigators – is money – money – money ... In Africa, the poor wretched natives – blessed with the most fertile and luxuriant soil – are rendered so much the more miserable for what Providence meant as a blessing: – the Christians' abominable traffic for slaves – and the horrid cruelty and treachery of the petty Kings – encouraged by their Christian customers ... But enough – it is a subject that sours my blood.

Source: Ignatius Sancho, *The Letters of the Late Ignatius Sancho, An African* (London, 1782, in two volumes; 5th edn, 1803, in one volume), Letter LXVIII, pp. 149–150.
See further: Ignatius Sancho, *Letters of the Late Ignatius Sancho, An African*, ed. Vincent Carretta (London, 1998), pp. 130–131.

QUOBNA OTTOBAH CUGOANO c. 1757–179?: Slavery and the slave trade contrary to the 'Law of God' 1787

Quobna Ottobah Cugoano was born in a Fante village on the coast of what is now Ghana. When he was about thirteen years old he was kidnapped and sold into slavery to European traders who shipped him to the West Indies. After a year or two his master took him to England in 1772. It is not known how Cugoano gained his freedom, but by the mid-1780s he was employed as a servant by the painters Richard and Maria Cosway of Pall Mall, London. Somehow he had also gained a very good education. Cugoano opposed the slave trade, but unlike most abolitionists he also demanded an end to slavery, which he denounced in his book, published in 1787. The book went into three editions and a French translation was published in Paris in 1788. A shorter version entitled *Thoughts and Sentiments on the Evil of Slavery* appeared in 1791. Little is known thereafter of Cugoano and he may have died in the early 1790s. These extracts from his first book firmly condemn the slave trade and slavery as contrary to the 'Law of God'.

But the whole business of slavery is an evil of the first magnitude, and a most horrible iniquity to traffic with slaves and souls of men; and an evil ... for sure the depredators, robbers and ensnarers of men can never be Christians, but ought to be held as the abhorrence of all men, and the abomination of all mankind, whether Christians or heathens ... And surely those men must be lost to all sensibility themselves, who can think that the stealing, robbing, enslaving, and murdering of men can be no crimes; but the holders of men in slavery are at the head of all these oppressions and crimes.

... the pretence that some men make use of for holding of slaves,

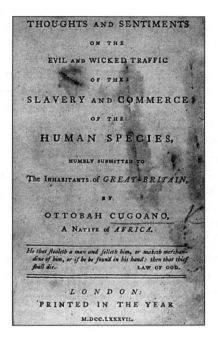

THOUGHTS AND SENTIMENTS

ON THE

EVIL AND WICKED TRAFFIC

OF THE

SLAVERY AND COMMERCE

OF THE

HUMAN SPECIES,

HUMBLY SUBMITTED TO

The INHABITANTS of *GREAT BRITAIN*,

BY

OTTOBAH CUGOANO,

A NATIVE of *AFRICA.*

He that stealeth a man and selleth him, or maketh merchandize of him, or if he be found in his hand; then that thief shall die. LAW OF GOD.

L O N D O N:

PRINTED IN THE YEAR

M.DCC.LXXXVII.

In his *Thoughts and Sentiments*, published in 1787, **Ottobah Cugoana** used the Bible to denounce the 'evil and wicked traffic' of slavery. This is emphasized by the text, adapted from Exodus 21:16, that appears on the title page of his book.

must be evidently the grossest perversion of reason, as well as an inconsistent and diabolical use of the sacred writings.

But this will appear evident to all men that believe the scriptures, that every reason necessary is given that they should be believed; and, in this case, that they afford us this information: 'That all mankind did spring from one original, and that there are no different species among men. For God who made the world, hath made of one blood all the nations of men that dwell on the face of the earth.'[1] Wherefore we may justly infer, as there are no inferior species, but all of one blood and of one nature, that there does not an inferiority subsist, or depend, on their colour, features or form, whereby some men make a pretence to enslave others; and consequently, as they have all one creator, one original, made of one blood, and all brethren descended from one father, it never could be lawful and just for any nation, or people, to oppress and enslave another.

... there is nothing in nature, reason, and scripture can be found in any manner or way, to warrant the enslaving of black people more than others.

The whole law of God is founded upon love, and the two grand branches of it are these: *Thou shalt love the Lord thy God with all thy heart and with all thy soul; and thou shalt love thy neighbour as thyself.*[2] And so it was when man was first created and made: they were created male and female, and pronounced to be in the image of God, and, as his representative, to have dominion over the lower creation.

But it is just as great and as heinous a transgression of the law of God to steal, kidnap, buy, sell, and enslave any one of the Africans, as it would be to ensnare any other man in the same manner, let him be who he will.

Source: Quobna Ottobah Cugoano, *Thoughts and Sentiments on the Evil and Wicked Traffic of the Slavery and Commerce of the Human Species, humbly submitted to the Inhabitants of the United Kingdom* (London, 1787), pp. 23–25, 30–31, 54, 60–62.
See further: Quobna Ottobah Cugoano, *Thoughts and Sentiments on the Evil of Slavery*, ed. Vincent Carretta (London, 1999).

OLAUDAH EQUIANO: The middle passage

The *Interesting Narrative* by Olaudah Equiano, a freed slave, was published in London in two volumes in 1789. It went into many editions in English and other languages, and provided a unique first-hand account by an African of the dreadful middle passage across the Atlantic from West Africa to the Americas. Equiano was active in the movement to abolish the slave trade and his *Interesting Narrative* was intended to emphasize the brutalities of slaving. In this well-known passage Equiano describes his fears as a child on being taken on board the strange and terrifying slave ship. Recent research has thrown some doubt on Equiano's claim to have been born and enslaved in West Africa. New evidence indicates that he may have been born in the Carolinas in the British North American colonies. However, even if this were the case, it barely diminishes the horror of his account, which could have been based on stories that he heard from other slaves recently arrived in America. (See also pp. 43, 80.)

The first object which saluted my eyes when I arrived on the coast was the sea, and a slave-ship, which was then riding at anchor, and waiting for its cargo. These filled me with astonishment, which was soon converted into terror, which I am yet at a loss to describe, nor the then feelings of my mind. When I was carried on board I was immediately handled, and tossed up, to see if I were sound, by some of the crew; and I was now persuaded that I had gotten into a world of bad spirits, and that they were going to kill me. Their complexions too differing so much from ours, their long hair, and the language they spoke, which was very different from any I had ever heard, united to confirm me in this belief. Indeed, such were the horrors of my views and fears at the moment, that, if ten thousand worlds had been my own, I would have freely parted with them all to have exchanged my condition with that of the meanest slave in my own country. When I looked round the ship too, and saw a large furnace of copper boiling, and a multitude of black people of every description chained together, every one of their countenances expressing dejection and sorrow, I no longer doubted of my fate, and, quite overpowered with horror and anguish, I fell motionless on the deck and fainted ... I now saw myself deprived of all chance of returning to my native country, or even the least glimpse of hope of gaining the shore, which I now considered as friendly: and I even wished for my former slavery in preference to my present situation, which was filled with horrors of every kind, still heightened by my ignorance of what I was to undergo. I was not long suffered to indulge my grief, I was soon put down under the decks, and there I received such a salutation in my nostrils as I had never experienced in my life; so that with the loathsomeness of the stench, and crying together, I became so sick and low that I was not able to eat, nor had I the least desire to taste any thing. I now wished for the last friend, Death, to relieve me ...

... At last when the ship we were in had got in all her cargo, they made ready with many fearful noises, and we were all put under the deck, so that we could not see how they managed the vessel. But this disappointment was the least of my sorrow. The stench of the hold while we were on the coast was so intolerably loathsome that it was dangerous to remain there for any time, and some of us had been permitted to stay on the deck for the fresh air; but now that the whole ship's cargo were confined together, it became absolutely pestilential. The closeness of the place, and the heat of the climate, added to the number in the ship, which was so crowded that each had scarcely room to turn himself, almost suffocated us ... the air soon became unfit for respiration, from a variety of loathsome smells, and brought on a sickness among the slaves ... This wretched situation was again aggravated by the galling of the chains, now become insupportable; and the filth of the necessary tubs, into which the children often fell, and were almost suffocated. The shrieks of the women, and the groans of the dying, rendered the whole a scene of horror almost inconceivable ... Every circumstance I met with served only to render my state more painful, and heighten my apprehensions, and my opinion of the cruelty of the whites.

... O, ye nominal Christians! might not an African ask you, learned you this from your God? who says unto you, Do unto all men as you would men should do unto you? Is it not enough that we are torn from our country and friends to toil for your luxury and lust of gain? Must every tender feeling be likewise sacrificed to your avarice?

Source: Olaudah Equiano, *The Interesting Narrative of the Life of Olaudah Equiano, or Gustavus Vassa, The African. Written by Himself* (London: 9th edn, 1794), pp. 46–57.
See further: Olaudah Equiano, *The Interesting Narrative and Other Writings*, ed. Vincent Carretta (London, 1995).

OLAUDAH EQUIANO: Abolition activist 1792

Olaudah Equiano was active in the campaign to abolish the slave trade and also to settle poor black people from London in West Africa. While he was in Edinburgh in 1792 he attended the General Assembly of the Church of Scotland when it agreed unanimously to send a petition to the House of Lords urging the abolition of the slave trade. Equiano thanked the members of the Assembly in a letter to an Edinburgh newspaper.

PERMIT me, one of the oppressed natives of Africa, to offer you the warmest thanks of a heart glowing with gratitude on the unanimous decision of your debate of this day – It filled me with love towards you. It is no doubt the indispensable duty of every man, who is a friend to religion and humanity, to give his testimony against that iniquitous branch of commerce the slave trade. It does not often fall to the lot of individuals to contribute to so important a moral and religious duty, as

Olaudah Equiano's *Interesting Narrative* was published in London in two volumes in 1789; it went into many editions and several languages. This frontispiece from the English edition of 1794 shows Equiano making a clear statement of his Christian faith by holding a Bible open at Acts 4:12, where it says of Jesus Christ, 'Neither is there any salvation in any other; for there is none other name under heaven given among men, whereby we must be saved.'

that of putting an end to the practice which may, without exaggeration, be stiled one of the greatest evils now existing on the earth. – The Wise Man saith, 'Righteousness exalteth a nation, but sin is a reproach to any people.' Prov. Xiv. 34...

GUSTAVUS VASSA the African.

Source: *Edinburgh Evening Courant*, 26 May 1792.

Equiano was also involved with the London Corresponding Society, a radical political organization formed in January 1792, organized by and drawn from members who were mainly artisans and working men. The Society demanded fair and equal represent-ation of the people in Parliament; it also opposed the slave trade and slavery. Its first public statement declared that all men possessed 'unalienable Rights of Resistance to Oppression'. The Society's radical demands and its opposition to the war with France was met by government suppression. By 1794 government spies had penetrated the Society, and Thomas Hardy and other leaders were arrested and charged with treason. By 1799 the Society had effectively ceased to function. Little is known of Equiano's role in the London Corresponding Society, but he was a firm supporter, as this letter to Hardy indicates:

> My best Respect to my fellow members of your society. I hope they do yet increase. I do not hear in this place that there is any such societys – I think Mr. Alexr. Matthews in Glasgow told me that there was (or is) some there.

> Source: Vincent Carretta, *Equiano the African: Biography of a Self-Made Man* (Athens, GA, 2005), p. 349.

JOHN FREDERIC NAIMBANNA d. 1793:
African prince

John Frederic was the son of a chief in Sierra Leone who had close dealings with the black and white settlers who established the settlement of Freetown in the late 1780s. In 1791 the chief sent two of his sons to Europe to be educated. John Frederic came to London, and his brother went to France. In England, John Frederic, who was known as the 'Black Prince', stayed at the home of Henry Thornton[3] in Clapham, Surrey. Thornton was an evangel-ical Christian and abolitionist whose friends included Thomas Clarkson,[4] Granville Sharp,[5] and William Wilberforce.[6] John Frederic proved to be an eager student. But he was very conscious of being African and black and, as this extract shows, was quick to condemn in strong terms Europeans who paraded their supposed superiority or who degraded Africans. John Frederic returned to Africa in 1793 with plans to preach the gospel to his people, but died on arrival.

If a man should rob me of my money, I can forgive him; if a man should shoot at me, or try to stab me, I can forgive him; if a man should sell me and all my family to a slave-ship, so that we should pass all the rest of our days in the West Indies, I can forgive him; [but] if a man should take away the character of Black people all over the world; and once he has taken away their character, there is nothing he may not do to Black people ever after. That man, for instance, will beat Black men, and say, 'Oh, it is only a Black man, why should I not beat him?' That man will make slaves of Black people; for when he has taken away their character, he will say, 'Oh, they are only Black people – why should not I make them slaves?' That man will take away all the people of Africa, if he can catch them; and if you ask him, 'But why do you take away all these people?' he will say, 'Oh, they are only Black people – they are not like White people –why should I not take them?' That is the reason why I cannot forgive the man who takes away the character of the people of my country.

Source: Prince Hoare, *The Memoirs of Granville Sharp Esq. Composed from his own Manuscripts*, 2 vols (London, 1828), 2, p. 167.

MARY PRINCE 1788–183?: An appeal for liberty

Mary Prince was born in Bermuda, the 'property' of Charles Myners. She was sold from one master to another, many of whom were cruel and misused her, and taken to various islands in the Caribbean. Despite her harsh life Mary learned to read and write, and in 1817 she was baptized as a member of the Moravian Church. When Mary married a freeman without asking permission from her owner, John Woods, he removed her to Antigua. Two years later the Woods took Mary with them to England to look after their child. Their cruel behaviour towards Mary continued in London, and in 1828 she fled their home and sought help from missionaries and members of the Anti-Slavery Society. Mary's dilemma was that if she wanted to see her husband again she would have to return to the West Indies, but that would mean going back into slavery. Thomas Pringle (1789–1834), then secretary of the Anti-Slavery Society, employed Mary as a domestic servant, and in 1831 Mary dictated her narrative to Susanna Strickland (1803–85). It was published in 1831 and quickly went into three editions. Clearly it was intended as a piece of anti-slavery propaganda, but it also shows Mary as a self-reliant and sturdy individual who was prepared to act in order to secure her freedom.

> I still live in the hope that God will find a way to give me my liberty, and give me back to my husband. I endeavour to keep down my fretting, and leave all to Him, for he knows what is good for me better than I know myself. Yet, I must confess, I find it a hard and heavy task to do so.
>
> I am often much vexed, and I feel great sorrow when I hear some people in this country say, that the slaves do not need better usage, and do not want to be free. They believe the foreign people, who deceive them, and say slaves are happy. I say, Not so. How can slaves be happy when they have the halter round their neck and the whip upon their back? and are disgraced and thought no more of than beasts? – and are separated from their mothers, and husbands, and children, and sisters, just as cattle are sold and separated? Is it happiness for a driver in the field to take down his wife or sister or child, and strip them and whip them in such a disgraceful manner? – women that have had children exposed in the open field to shame! There is no modesty of decency shown by the owner to his slaves; men, women, and children are exposed alike. Since I have been here I have often wondered how English people can go into the West Indies and act in such a beastly manner. But when they go to the West Indies they forget God and all feeling of shame, I think, they can see and do such things.

Source: Mary Prince, *The History of Mary Prince, a West Indian Slave. Related by Herself* (London, 3rd edn, 1831).
See further: Mary Prince, *The History of Mary Prince*, ed. Sara Sahil (London, 2000).

ASHTON WARNER c. 1806–31: 'Freedom to the slaves'

Ashton Warner was born to slave parents on the Cane Grove estate in the island of St Vincent. When the estate changed hands, Warner's aunt bought and freed both Warner and his mother. The new owner refused to recognize Warner's manumission and kidnapped him. Warner was determined to gain his freedom, and in 1830 he escaped from the island and worked his passage to London, hoping to present his manumission papers to his former owner. Unfortunately that man had recently died and the estate was in the hands of executors. In late February 1831 Warner fell ill and died in the London Hospital of an 'inflammatory complaint', his last recorded words apparently being 'Freedom to the slaves'. Warner's account *Negro Slavery described by a Negro* was published in London shortly after his death.

> It is not from what I have suffered in my own body as a slave, that I wish to publish this narrative, for I was better off than thousands of my poor countrymen – but I wished to relate not only my own case, but also all that I know of slavery – all that I have heard with my own ears, and beheld with my own eyes – in the hope that it may help to make known the condition of the poor negroes to the English people, and stir them up to do away with slavery altogether.

> Source: S. Strickland, *Negro Slavery described by a Negro: being The Narrative of Ashton Warner, a Native of St. Vincent's* ... (London, 1831), pp. 63–64.

MOSES ROPER 1816–60s: Lecturing around Britain

Moses Roper was born on a slave plantation in North Carolina. He was frequently sold and moved all over the eastern parts of the southern states, witnessing many acts of brutality to fellow slaves. Roper made several unsuccessful attempts to escape, but eventually in 1834 he fled and reached Savannah. He worked there for a year and then sailed to Britain. He became widely known as the first slave to escape to Britain from slavery in the United States. Moses Roper's *Narrative* was widely read and by 1856 had appeared in ten editions. Strictly speaking Roper was not 'a Black British' writer. However, he is included here because his public appearances and speeches made throughout the British Isles were important in helping to promote the abolitionist cause in Britain.

BERWICK, MARCH, 1846.

> SOON after my arrival in England, I went to a boarding-school at Hackney, near London, and afterwards to another boarding-school at

Wallingford, and after learning to read and write and some other
branches, I entered as a student at University College, London, which
place, I very much regret, however, I was obliged to leave, in consequence
of bad health; and during the time I was at school I lectured in different
towns and sold my Narrative or book to pay for my education. On the
29th of December, 1839, I was married to a lady of Bristol, and, after
travelling tens of thousands of miles, and lecturing in nearly every town
and hundreds of villages in England, at the commencement of 1844, I left
England with my family for British North America, and have taken up my
future residence in Canada West, it being as near as I can get to my
relations (who are still in bondage) without being again taken. Having
some matters of a private nature to settle in this country, I left Canada in
December, 1845, for England, and arrived at Liverpool, on the 25th of
January, 1846, in the ship Orphan. I intend now, before I return to
Canada, to visit Scotland and Ireland, and deliver lectures, as I have not
been in many towns in those countries. I shall then bid farewell once
more to dear and happy Old England, not expecting again ever to return,
but hoping to meet many thousands of her inhabitants (whom I have seen
and addressed) in Heaven. My dear and kind friends, throughout Great
Britain and Ireland, farewell!

Source: Moses Roper, *Narrative of the Adventures and Escapes of Moses Roper,
from American Slavery* ... (Berwick-upon-Tweed, 1848), Appendix.
See further: David A. Davis, Tampathia Evans, Ian Frederick Finseth and
Andrea N. Williams, eds., *North Carolina Slave Narratives: The Lives of Moses
Roper, Lunsford Lane, Moses Grandy and Thomas H. Jones* (Chapel Hill, NC,
2005).

ANON:
A poem to Moses Roper: 'The glorious work of liberty'

Moses Roper not only wrote a book about his escape from US
slavery but he travelled all over Britain speaking in churches and
chapels in support of the abolitionist cause. In 1844 he returned
across the Atlantic to live in Canada. He made a further visit to
Britain in 1848. An edition of his *Narrative*, published in Berwick in
1848, contained several (not very good) poems written by British
supporters, one being by an unidentified black Briton whom Roper
met on his travels in central Scotland.

TO MR. MOSES ROPER.

VERSES WRITTEN IMPROMPTU BY A MAN OF COLOUR,
ON MEETING MR. ROPER IN THE VALE OF LEVEN,
DUMBARTONSHIRE.

Thank Heaven, I have lived to see begun,
And consummated nearly, I may say,
The glorious work of Liberty, – whose sun
Has usher'd in the smile of risen day...

But oh! my country! must thou still remain
To wear thy fetters – and degraded be?
When shall be torn the galling cruel chain?
Must thou be doom'd to endless slavery?

No! thou art class'd already among the free –
See thy warm advocate, young Roper, stand!
In love's sweet embassy most powerfully
He breaks thy chain, with mighty giant hand.

His tyrant follows with his bloody hounds,
The track is lost – he plunges in the wave;
And now with fleetest speed onward he bounds,
And from him throws the cursed brand of slave.

Heaven throws its shield around thee, gallant youth,
With open arms, lo! Britain doth thee hail,
Long shall its ministers thy sorrows soothe,
And hear with interest thy affecting tale.

August 30, 1838.

Source: Moses Roper, *Narrative of the Adventures and Escapes of
Moses Roper, from American Slavery* ... (Berwick-upon-Tweed, 1848),
p. 60.

HENRY BECKFORD: An international delegate to the World Anti-Slavery Convention 1840

Edward Barrett and Henry Beckford were both born into slavery in Jamaica. Both men became Christians while they were slaves. Both men also became deacons, Barrett[7] in the church of the Baptist missionary Revd William Knibb[8] in Falmouth, and Beckford at St Ann's. In 1840, together with Knibb, they came to Britain as western Jamaica's delegates to the World Anti-Slavery Convention that met in London in June. The Convention was an international gathering, organized by the British and Foreign Anti-Slavery Society (BFASS), which campaigned to end slavery throughout the world. William Knibb was well known in Britain for his campaigns against slavery, and a large meeting was held in Birmingham town hall to welcome him home in May 1840. At that meeting Barrett and Beckford spoke to an audience of 5,000 people.[9] The next month Beckford spoke at the London Convention, following an opening speech by Thomas Clarkson, the veteran campaigner against the slave trade and slavery. In a painting of the Convention by Benjamin Haydon, Beckford is seated in the foreground beneath Clarkson. In the next few months, Knibb, Barrett and Beckford toured Britain speaking on platforms throughout the country. The two black Christians were held up as prime examples of emancipated slaves, and, in the words of Catherine Hall, as 'archetypical new black subjects' of the Empire.

Mr. HENRY BECKFORD, (of Jamaica). – I pray God to look down in mercy upon the labours of this Society, which has been formed in this country to deliver us from bondage. I rejoice to see the kind gentleman who, as the root of this Society, relieved my body from suffering. I rejoice to tender my thanks to the British ladies from one end of the land to the other. I have seen the blood run down the negro's back; I have seen the poor creatures confined in chains; but how shall I rejoice when I return to my native country, to tell my friends that I have seen those gentlemen who delivered us from the accursed system which was the ruin of men's souls as well as their bodies! Slavery brought men down to the level of four-footed beasts; but now, when I return, no man can ask me where I have been. I came here as a freeman, and I shall return as the same. I was a slave for twenty-eight years, but look at me and work on. There are other parts of the world where slavery now exists, but I trust the negroes there will soon become freemen as I am to-day. We hope, however, that you will assist us till we become more thoroughly established in the blessings we now enjoy, and we will assist you by our prayers till slavery is abolished throughout the world. I hope that this assembly will enjoy the blessing of God, and that great benefits will result from your deliberations. It is good to be the servants of the Lord Jesus Christ, and to be engaged in promoting His cause.

Source: *Proceedings of the Anti-Slavery Convention 1840* (London, 1841), pp. 22–23.

See further: Catherine Hall, *Civilising Subjects: Metropole and Colony in the English Imagination 1830–1867* (Oxford, 2002).

ROBERT GORDON 1830–?: Racism in a colonial church

From an early age Robert Gordon, a free black born in Jamaica, felt called to become a priest in the Church of England in his home island. The Anglican Church was dominated by the white planter class and from 1825 successive bishops excluded black men from becoming clergy. When Gordon applied to become a priest in 1853, he recalled, 'As it has ever been the policy of the Jamaican church to exclude the black man from preaching the Gospel, obstacles were ever after studiously raised to prevent the realization of my object.' It was suggested that Gordon train in Barbados in order to go to Africa as a missionary. He refused, feeling that his calling was to work among his own people in Jamaica. In 1857 Gordon went to England, undertook some training, and then was appointed to a mission in Canada, where he was ordained. Returning to Jamaica he unsuccessfully applied to be employed as a priest. From 1862 to 1867, Gordon was the elected head-master of Wolmer's Grammar School in Kingston. In 1867 he sailed for England, where he was licensed by the Archbishop of Canterbury. In the early 1870s, when he was curate at St John-at-Wapping, in East London, Gordon wrote a pamphlet, addressed to the colonial secretary, Lord Kimberley, explaining how racist attitudes had weakened the ministry of the Anglican Church in Jamaica.

I hold that the Anglo-Saxon race having, during many generations, used
their superior knowledge and physical power in injuring, oppressing, and
degrading the black race, it is their moral duty to do everything in their
power now that slavery has been abolished in the countries which their
'auri sacra fames' ['accursed hunger for gold'] had caused to have been its
miserable strongholds – to assist in elevating them to whatever stations
in life they may have all the qualifications for filling with honour to
themselves and advantage to society; at any rate, to place no insuperable
bar in their way, on the ground of colour, for which you and I, my Lord
[Kimberley], are just as responsible as for the changeable weather that
we have been experiencing from the beginning of the year. The hateful
policy of the Jamaican Church, persistently carried out by the Bishop of
Kingston, has ever been to make an invidious distinction between the
white and coloured subjects of Her Majesty, and the black inhabitants,
who are as loyal to the British Throne and Constitution as are any of the
former, in the systematic exclusion from the ministry of any candidate of
pure Negro origin, thereby nullifying an important part of the political,
social, and legal rights of three-fourths of the population.

Source: Robert Gordon, *The Jamaica Church: Why It Has Failed* (London,
n.d., c. 1872), p. 6.
See further: Robert J. Stewart, *Religion and Society in Post-Emancipation
Jamaica* (Knoxville, TN, 1992), pp. 94–109.

CHARLOTTE MANYE 1871–1939: A plea for racial equality
Charlotte Manye was born in the eastern region of the British Cape
Colony in South Africa. Both her parents were Christians, her father
being a local preacher. Charlotte attended a mission school and then
became a teacher in a Wesleyan school in Kimberley. She spoke
Sotho, Xhosa, Dutch, English and Afrikaans, and was a gifted
singer. In 1890 Charlotte joined the all-black African Choir. The
Choir, inspired by the example of African American choirs such as
the Fisk Jubilee Singers, hoped by similar public performances to
raise money for an industrial school in South Africa. The African
Choir successfully toured Cape Colony before embarking in April
1891 for a tour of Britain. It appeared all over the country, and sang
before Queen Victoria. However, the British tour was not a success
and the choir ended up heavily in debt. A further tour of the United

States in 1894 was also a financial failure. Charlotte remained in America to study at the African American Wilberforce University in Ohio, where she married a fellow South African, the Revd Marshall Maxeke of the African Methodist Episcopal Church. After they returned home to South Africa, Charlotte was a Christian social worker and teacher and also an active member of the African National Congress.

Cape Colony was a British territory but racial policies discriminated against black people. Many educated Africans regarded themselves as British and argued that they were entitled to equal treatment under the law as white people. The difference between South African policies towards Africans compared to those in Britain was pointed out by Charlotte in an interview published in the London liberal monthly journal the *Review of Reviews* in September 1891.

> Let us be in Africa even as we are in England. Here we are treated as men and women. Yonder we are but as cattle. But in Africa, as in England, we are human. Can you not make your people at the Cape as kind and just as your people here? That is the first thing and the greatest. But there are still three other things that I would ask. Help us to found the schools for which we pray where our people could learn to labour, to build, to acquire your skill with their hands. Then could we be sufficient unto ourselves. Our young men would build us houses and lay out our farms, and our tribes would develop independently of the civilisation and industries which you have given us. Thirdly, give our children free education. Fourthly, shut up the canteens, and take away the drink. These four things we ask from the English. Do not say us nay.

Source: *Review of Reviews*, 4.2 (September 1891), p. 256.
See further: Veit Erlmann, *Music, Modernity, and the Global Imagination: South Africa and the West* (New York, 1999).

THEOPHILUS SCHOLES c. 1858–c. 1940s:
Protest at lynching

Theophilus E. S. Scholes was born and grew up in St Ann's, Jamaica. He became a seaman, visited the United States, and then trained as a doctor in Scotland. Scholes was a medical missionary in the Congo from 1886 to 1888, took an MD degree at Brussels in

1893, and in the following year he was at the Alfred Jones Institute at Buguma in New Calabar, southern Nigeria. Increasingly he opposed colonial rule and the growing racial discrimination that accompanied it. In this letter from Scholes, published in London in *Fraternity*, the journal of the Society for the Recognition of the Brotherhood of Man, he condemns the lynching of black people in the United States and compares it with the mass murder of Armenians in the Ottoman Empire. (See also pp. 95, 114.)

> Recently the picture of Armenian villages drenched in blood, strewed with the corpses of strong men, resounding with the shrieks of outraged women, and the ribald shouts of a brutal soldiery, convulsed the civilized world with horror. But let us turn to another picture – a woman lynched. [Scholes then describes the brutal murder in the United States of an African American woman who was accused of murdering a white child.] To understand the full significance of this picture, we must regard it as the representation of over two thousand similar scenes, narrated within the same limit of time as that comprised by the Armenian atrocities, and, with the same fullness of detail. I aver that we have here, under the Stars and Stripes, a record of malice and cruelty as unrelenting, as inhuman and as fiendish, as those which recently stained the Crescent,[10] and scandalized humanity.
>
> ... we are astounded at the enormous activity expounded by some of the foremost men and women of America in attempting to cure the social ills of other nations. And yet, except for the annual passing of a few colourless resolutions, no united or pronounced attempt is made to raise the prostrate law to health and efficiency ... But if all of these great and good people were to join their forces at home for a brief season, to secure for the law of the land its due supremacy, would these American atrocities continue to pollute the morals of the nation?
>
> Source: *Fraternity*, 1 June 1896, p. 156.

By 1898 Scholes was back in Britain and he turned his hand to writing books on political topics, including studies of British imperial trade. In 1897 a Royal Commission reported on the declining sugar industry of the British West Indian islands. Scholes wrote a book on the subject. In this next extract he condemns the

use of women in the hard labour of road-building for low wages in
colonial Jamaica.

> Women, too, experience difficulty in getting work; one form of outdoor
> labour that attracts female workers is the breaking of stones for
> macadamizing public roads: at this, a woman has first to collect the stone
> which may be found in sufficient quantities on the hill-tops of varying
> heights; and when they are rolled down to the level, where in the broiling
> sun, and with a hammer of two pound weight they are broken. The
> broken stones are then measured in four-barrels, and for each barrel the
> woman receives three-pence.

Source: T. E. S. Scholes, *Sugar and the West Indies* (London, 1898), p. 4.

Little is known of Scholes's private life and beliefs after the late
1890s. He was certainly outraged that many Christians viewed black
people with prejudice. In Africa he had experienced the con-
temptuous attitudes of white missionaries and also seen the way in
which African Christians were treated as inferiors. In this extract
he indicates how many black people became disillusioned with
Christianity because of the prejudice of white people and church
leaders. It is not known when Scholes died, but it was probably in
Britain some time in the late 1930s or early 1940s. His last known
piece of writing was in 1920.

> 'God has made of one blood all nations of men, for to dwell on all the
> earth; and hath determined the times before appointed, and the bounds
> of their habitation.'[11] Under these, her Golden Rules and Marching
> Orders, may not the Ethiopian[12] be sure to find in the Christian Church
> that solace, and succour, and brotherly confidence, which are denied him
> both by Politics and by Literature?
>
> In theory the Ethiopian does receive the Christian protection. But the
> Church fails to carry her theory fully out into practice. And this is
> especially true of the Protestant section of the Church. If the Church had
> fully recognised the Ethiopian as 'a man and a brother,' Politics and
> Literature would have done so likewise, for in this respect at least they
> would reflect the action of the Church. We must not be thought to mean
> that *all* Christians, in both hemispheres, hold and practice the unchristian

sentiments of race hatred and race distinctions, but we do wish to state
our conviction that the solid mass of them do.

Source: Theophilus E. S. Scholes, *The British Empire and Alliances* (London,
1899), pp. 288–290.

J. EDMESTONE BARNES c. 1860s–c. 1920s:
Prophetic ideas

Dispensationalist ideas – about the last times and the return of
Christ – are commonly held by many Christians in the United States
today. In the first thirty years of the twentieth century similar ideas
were also popular among some British Christians, who believed the
British Empire would have a major role in the final confrontation
between nations before the second coming. These millennialist
views, based on a particular reading of Old Testament prophecies
and the New Testament Revelation, were applied to present times.
In 1903, J. Edmestone Barnes did just that when he predicted a war
in 1908–10 between Britain and continental Europe led by a
Russian-French-German alliance. Barnes was born in Barbados in
1857 and had travelled widely as a surveyor and engineer in South
America and Africa. Barnes wrote several brief books, and travelled
to the United States, where he condemned the use of the word
'Negro'. For much of his life he lived in Britain.

> ...modern, Germany – [is] the Magog of Ezekiel ... 'Gog of the
> Magog – Prince Rosh of Meschech and Tubal' is modern Russia in all its
> magnitude and greatness ... 'Gomer' – France or the French Republic.
> The alliance between Russia and France exists: and there is also a secret
> alliance between Russia and Germany...
>
> But Ezekiel also speaks of another very formidable adversary of another
> part, on the other hand, who will meet Gog and his hosts in the appointed
> battlefield at the appointed time, and give him apparently more hard work
> to do than Gog and his hosts have ever dreamed of, or contemplated. In
> fact, according to the signs, this power seemed to be destined to accomplish
> the most marvellous things that will ever be transacted by a nation upon the
> earth, at least in this aeon ... In modern phraseology that power is Great
> Britain of Europe and Greater Britain beyond the seas combined.[13]
>
> From the foregoing, the handwriting on the wall is for every Briton,

be he white or black, red or blue, at no distant date will be required to do duty to the Empire's cause ... the Powers, great and small, have resolved themselves into two hostile parties – Gog, or Russia, at the head of all the armies and navies of Continental Europe on the one hand, and Great Britain of Europe, and the dominions Greater Britain beyond the seas, on the other hand, combined, will be gathered together by the force of circumstances in battle array, to decide who shall subdue and vanquish the other, and become the chief of the European and Oriental Cosmos. It will be a struggle as described, such as never was since there was a nation upon the earth to the present day.

Source: J. Edmestone Barnes, *The Signs of the Times Touching the Final Supremacy of Nations* (London, 1903), pp. 38, 43–44.

THEOPHILUS SCHOLES: Racial equality

When Theophilus Scholes returned to Britain from Africa (see pp. 91–93), he turned to writing books critical of British imperial activity and of racial discrimination. In two lengthy volumes, he set out to show that all humanity had common physical, mental, and moral attributes. (See also p. 114.)

Primarily man sustains a threefold relation. A relation to his Maker, a relation to his fellows, and a relation to the material world ... these relations carry with them corresponding obligations. And in the case of man and man ... these obligations are discharged in conformity to a law, which is expressed in the words, 'Thou shalt love thy neighbour as thyself'; or 'Do unto others as ye would they should do unto you' ... so no man on this planet escapes the obligation to this law of goodness...

Reduced to their final limits, the dealings of the colourless race[14] with the coloured races of the British Empire, give us a series of three wrongs. The first wrong is that of forcing the coloured races into the Empire ... The second wrong is that after these coloured races ... had bestowed upon the Empire their enforced and unrequited toil, and ... the revenues towards the support of their numerous governments, the hegemonical state [promised but denied them] that they should be accorded equality of treatment with the colourless race, and should be prepared for autonomous government ... And the third wrong is that ... the hegemonical state, endeavours to justify its unfaithfulness to these races ... by means of oppressive taxation, defective educational facilities, and every form of obstruction which is placed in their way, by the systematic aspersion of their character with lies of the most abominable kind, and by degrading, humiliating, and deceiving them.

Source: Samuel E. Theophilus Scholes, *Glimpses of the Ages or the 'Superior' and 'Inferior' Races, So-called, Discussed in the Light of Science and History*, 2 (London, 1908), pp. 475, 486–488.

JOHN EDWARD QUINLAN c. 1860s–c. 1920s:
The unity of humanity

Little is known about John Edward Quinlan or his religious faith. He was born in St Lucia in the West Indies and trained as a land surveyor. Quinlan came to Britain to attend the 1900 Pan-African Conference in London. Two years later he published a brief book outlining his socialist ideas, *The Labour Problem: An Idea of a British Workers' Society* (London, 1902), in which he argued for support for Labour Members of Parliament and that British workers should 'return one or two dark Colonials as members of the House of Commons'. In 1906 Quinlan founded the National Society for the Protection of the Dark Races. This organization seems to have faded within a short time; only a single issue exists of its ten-page journal, *The Telephone*. On the front page of the journal there is a photograph of Quinlan and the biblical verse which was the motto of the National Society. In this extract Quinlan elaborates on that text by emphasizing that true Christianity stresses the unity of all humanity.

GOD HATH MADE OF ONE BLOOD ALL NATIONS OF MEN
(Acts xvii, 26)

These true and memorable words, uttered by St. Paul the Apostle when addressing from Mars Hill[15] the inhabitants of the most intellectual city of his time, Athens, are taken as a suitable motto for the Journal of the National Society for the Protection of Dark Races, which we are proud to issue from the very heart of the Empire, – London, – the largest and most remarkable city ever known in the history of man.

Jesus Christ knew no sect. He condemned sectarianism in words impossible to be misunderstood. Jesus Christ knew no caste. He

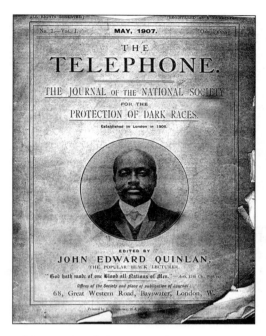

No. 1.—Vol. I.   MAY, 1907.   ONE PENNY

THE

TELEPHONE.

THE JOURNAL OF THE NATIONAL SOCIETY
FOR THE
PROTECTION OF DARK RACES.

Established in London in 1906.

EDITED BY
JOHN EDWARD QUINLAN,
THE POPULAR BLACK LECTURER.
"God hath made of one Blood all Nations of Men."—Acts, 17th Ch. 26th ver.
Offices of the Society and place of publication of Journal :
68, Great Western Road, Bayswater, London, W.

John Edward Quinlan attended the Pan-African Congress in London in
1900. Little is known of his National Society for the Protection of Dark
Races, founded in London in 1906; only one issue of its journal, *The
Telephone*, seems to have been published.

> condemned caste in language eloquent in its vituperation and
> unanswerable in its logic and clearness.
>   The Christianity of Jesus and of St. Paul was significantly
> cosmopolitan. It was this Cosmopolitan principle in the teaching of
> Jesus that offended the haughty Pharisees; it was the same principle in
> the teaching of St. Paul that bewildered the learned Athenians. But in this
> cosmopolitanism of Christianity lies its greatness and the hope of the
> world. In other words, the Christianity of Jesus, for the first time in the
> history of the world, enunciated the great new principle of the
> brotherhood of man, whatever be his colour or his race, and the great
> Eternal Power is the father of them all. Such was the principle running
> through all the teachings of Jesus, and was taken up by St. Paul and other
> early teachers and promulgated with all the enthusiasm of good men
> possessed of a new great idea...

There are unfortunately some dwellers in the British Isles, and large numbers of ... professing Christians of the fair complexion in various parts of the world, who refuse to admit the truth of these words of the Apostle. They even go further and invoke the aid of Science, so called, against the principle preached so eloquently by St. Paul on Mars Hill, claiming, as they do, that members of their race are of a superior type and not of the same blood as those of a dark complexion ... 'God hath made of one blood all nations of men.'

Source: *The Telephone*, Journal of the Society for the Protection of the Dark Races, 1 (May 1907), pp. 3–4.

A. B. C. MERRIMAN-LABOR c. 1870s–c. 1920s:
Racial discrimination in Edwardian Britain

Merriman-Labor came from West Africa to London in 1904. His purpose was to study law and also to write. He described some of his experiences in London, including racial discrimination combined with abuse and rudeness. In this extract from his book he describes how he dealt with vulgar white Americans who objected to his presence in the dining room of a London hotel where he was staying. (See also pp. 99, 100, 130.)

[A newspaper has asked] 'Should Negroes use the same restaurant with Europeans'? My answer would have been embodied in a description of the following incident which I experienced at a hotel in Bloomsbury where I was once staying as a permanent lodger. Some Euro-Americans who met me there objected to sit at table with me. The proprietor, in order to please them, asked me to alter my meal time. I told him I was not prepared to change my meal time one second to please them or the likes of their kidney. I further told the Euro-Americans concerned that as I was a permanent lodger and a British subject, I had better right to that hotel and better right in this country than any of them. That was the end of the matter. They altered their meal time which, of course, they had a perfect right to do.

Source: A. B. C. Merriman-Labor, *Britons Through Negro Spectacles* (London, 1909), pp. 118–119.

A. B. C. MERRIMAN-LABOR: Schools and educational opportunities in Britain and West Africa

From the mid-nineteenth century onwards, a small but steady stream of young men and women came to Britain from the Caribbean and West African colonies to study in universities and colleges. Most of these students were from elite families and they already had received a good level of education in local schools, most run by Christian missions, that qualified them to enter universities in Britain to study medicine, law or theology. Merriman-Labor's remarks on British education were largely motivated by his experience of British official disdain for educated Africans in West Africa. Along with a number of other West Africans, Merriman-Labor claimed that European civilization was largely derived from Africa, and that the Cushites mentioned in the book of Genesis were Africans who taught 'the elementary principles of government to the Egyptians, from whom Greece and ... Rome ... Europe and America borrowed much that was profitable'.[16] He argued that African languages and history should be included in the curriculum of West African schools. (See also p. 100.)

Irrespective of the religious training, and with regard to elementary education generally, it seems to me that the aim of the authorities in Britain, is merely to give the child a good groundwork in reading, 'riting, and 'rithmetic, or the 'three R's,' as these three subjects were once enumerated and explained in a speech by an illiterate alderman of the City of London. On the other hand, in addition to these subjects, the missionary societies thrust into the heads of the elementary school child in West Africa, all the knotty names in the Bible, more knotty ones in British history and geography, and the thousand and one meaningless rules in English grammar.

Poor soul! I wish his well-meant teachers had taught him more of some grammars of African languages, more of African history and geography, and less of British subjects. His teachers, notwithstanding, had an eye to his well-being. The missionaries have imparted to the West African a British education which, though defective, possesses more good points than one.

Such education admits, besides other advantages, of a possibility of comparison between the training of the British elementary scholar on the one side, and his prototype in West Africa on the other.

This comparison I could make easily [from experience as a school teacher in the Gambia and a Sunday school teacher in south London] ... [as] these different capacities teach me ... that, broadly speaking, the black child has, on leaving school, more book learning in his head than a white one, when the already enumerated subjects, not excluding the three R's, are considered. A black child fresh from school knows, as a rule, in regard to Bible, geography and history facts, not to mention grammar rules, more than two white children put together, although he may not be as graceful in practical English composition as one white child.

Source: A. B. C. Merriman-Labor, *Britons Through Negro Spectacles* (London, 1909), pp. 143–147.

A. B. C. MERRIMAN-LABOR: The social and political position of British women and of black peoples

At the time when Merriman-Labor was writing, many women in Britain were struggling to get the vote and other civil rights that were denied to them. In this extract he drew a parallel between the then position of British women and that of Africans in the colonies, from which black people might draw some lessons. (See also p. 130.)

Because advanced British women clamour for equal political and social rights in a country where they own land and other property, some white men try to spoil their cause by representing that women are by nature intellectually, physically, morally, and socially inferior to men. The very same malrepresentation, word for word, has been made concerning advanced British Negroes when they ask for equal political and, it may be, equal social rights in their own country. But the representation against British women and British Negroes, as well as those against other women and other Negroes, are wrong, foolish, and wicked ...

Women and Negroes are not by nature intellectually inferior. At schools, they always pass the same examinations as, and not infrequently, better examinations than white men ... Women and Negroes are not by nature physically inferior. It has been said that the latter though strong for primitive life, are not equal to the exactitudes of civilised conditions.

If British women are trained properly, they will become as strong as women in the interior of Africa who always go farming or hunting the very day they give birth ... Women and Negroes are not by nature morally inferior. The findings of psychologists about the average woman are that she is morally stronger than the average man. Psychologists say that most women for months can be quite indifferent to yearnings with which men daily torture themselves...

As regards the alleged moral inferiority of Negroes, I say it is a lie...

Women and Negroes are not by nature socially inferior ... the more advanced ones know that nature did not intend them to be slaves to white men ... The agitative British women are therefore rightly striving for equal political and social rights in their own country.[17] The agitative British Negroes want equal rights, if not social rights as well, in their own country.

Source: A. B. C. Merriman-Labor, *Britons Through Negro Spectacles* (London, 1909), pp. 206–210.

FELIX E. M. HERCULES 1882–1943:
The spirit of black nationalism

Felix Eugene Michael Hercules grew up in Trinidad. He came to Britain during the First World War and studied at London University. His experiences of racism left him disillusioned with 'Christian Britain'. Instead of the charity and warmth that he had expected, he encountered the harsh face of the 'colour bar'. Although in many ways conservative, Hercules became racially radical. In 1918 he became secretary-general of the Society of Peoples of African Origin (SPAO). Later he took a leading part in the African Progress Union and it was largely due to him that these two pan-Africanist bodies came together in 1919. In 1917 or early 1918 Hercules met the Sierra Leonean businessman J. Eldred Taylor, who invited him to become editor of his revived newspaper *The African Telegraph*. In his brief period as editor, Hercules made the *Telegraph* more outspokenly pan-Africanist, condemning racial discrimination in Britain and in the colonies, with some of his harshest condemnation directed at whites who started race riots in major British cities in 1919. In mid-1919 Hercules was sent by the SPAO to tour the West Indies to recruit members and gather

information. He was closely watched by the colonial authorities. In
1920 he went to New York, where he was briefly involved in African
American politics. He then became a Baptist minister and had
pastorates in Arkansas, Tennessee, and Illinois. Felix Hercules died
in Chicago in 1943.

What is required is the development of a healthy African spirit. Time was
when I deemed myself an Internationalist. *Then* I deprecated every
manifestation of national feeling, as a breach of a canon of good taste;
I was groping blindly for a 'something' that would transcend mere
nationality, searching after the elusive 'something' in humanity that would
help men to meet in common and to remain linked without being
narrowed by paltry considerations of political frontiers and geographical
barriers. If I had never come to England I might even now be an
Internationalist. But England, with its barriers and its prejudices, its caste
system as rigid as any practised by the Hindoos; Western civilisation with
its sham and hypocrisy, with its conventionalities and its deification of
Money and Force where one hoped to find Christ, these things it is that
have driven me to the refuge of my own people ... And yet I have
remained sufficiently catholic to believe that the day will surely come
when men of every nationality and of every race will look back of colour,
back of superficial differences, and see clearly the brotherhood in man
and the resemblances where now they see only differences because their
judgment is warped by some mental obliquity.

    I cannot see how Africans can hope to receive fair treatment until
national spirit has become instinctive amongst us. Have Africans done
nothing down the ages which we may to-day recall with pride? ... We
were created Africans that we might re-create Africa; the responsibility is
not one we can shirk. This age is one of Nationalism ... [but Africans]
are not a militarist or an aggressive people, our evolution proceeds rather
along the line of peace ... This is the spirit we must acquire and foster:
the spirit that puts Africa and service to Africa first ... the spirit whose
realisation will confer upon us and our country political adulthood,
recognition, self-determination ... Africa, thy sons may be *backward*; they
are not *degenerate*; thy children may be *undeveloped* but they are not *unmindful*
of thee. Great Mother, we are closing up our ranks: we are coming!

Source: *The African Telegraph*, September–October 1919, p. 84.

SOLOMON PLAATJE 1876–1932: A plea for African rights

Sol Plaatje was a founder member of the South African Native National Congress (SANNC)[18] and, like many of its early members, an active Christian. He was born in the Orange Free State and educated in mission schools, and became a civil servant. Plaatje was fluent in several African and European languages. In 1914 he came to Britain with a SANNC delegation to protest at the recent Land Act passed by the Parliament of the newly created white-dominated Union of South Africa.[19] Plaatje's appeal was that Africans were British subjects whose rights were being taken away. While in Britain Plaatje spoke frequently on public platforms about the wrongs inflicted on Africans. In 1916 he had published a book on the Land Act, an appeal to the British public, which opened with the words, *'Awakening on Friday morning, June 20, 1913, the South African Native found himself, not actually a slave, but a pariah in the land of his birth.'* The pleas of the SANNC delegation fell empty on official ears. Plaatje returned to Britain again in 1919 with a further delegation from the SANNC. This time he published a pamphlet which listed the evils of racial segregation imposed on Africans by the South African government. Here is a section from it.

(a) In Cape Colony (where Natives have exercised the franchise[20] for sixty years) coloured voters may not now elect a man of colour to represent them in the legislative assembly. No Native taxpayer is entitled to a vote in Transvaal, Orange Free State or Natal...

(b) Coloured persons are excluded by act of Parliament from membership rights in the Dutch Reformed Church outside Cape Colony...

(c) Coloured mechanics are precluded from working as skilled labourers in the industrial centres...

(d) Coloured citizens are excluded from military training in the citizens' defence force...

(e) The settlement of Europeans on crown land and the establishment of a land bank to advance state funds to white farmers is limited to Europeans...

(f) Native miners are not allowed to benefit by the pensions and other advantages provided by law for miners who contract miners' phthisis...

(g)   Natives are prohibited from buying fixed property ... except in
      tribal locations, that are already overcrowded...

(i)   Native passengers holding tickets are not allowed to travel in any
      train other than in a Native compartment...

(j)   Natives, whatever their qualification may be, are not employed in
      the public service except as 'casual' menial labourers...

Source: Sol Plaatje, *Some of the Legal Disabilities Suffered by the Native
Population of the Union of South Africa and Imperial Responsibility* (London,
1919).
See further: Brian Willan, ed., *Sol Plaatje: Selected Writings* (Johannesburg,
1996), pp. 20–22, and Brian Willan, *Sol Plaatje: South African Nationalist
1876–1932* (London, 1984).

HAROLD MOODY 1882–1947: The League of Coloured Peoples: Christian purpose and pacifism

From his home in south London, Dr Harold Moody in 1931 helped
found the League of Coloured Peoples (LCP) and became its
president. His idea was that the League would become the main
body representing the interests of black people – those of African
origin and descent – in Britain. In its early years the League was
engaged more in welfare issues than in overt political ones. But even
welfare activities caused division – between West Africans and West
Indians, between young and old, and between cautious liberals, like
Moody, and those who wanted the League to be politically active
and left-wing. Moody's support for an officially run black student
hostel in London, Aggrey House, was condemned by the West
African Students' Union. The 'African and West Indian bickering
among themselves about things which do not matter', the 'petty
jealousies and childish petulance' that undermined the 'good of the
race' made Moody despair. In the October issue of *The Keys*, the
journal of the League, he announced that he would cease being
president. However, he reasserted his control over the League, and
agreed to stand for election as president. Here is his speech to the
annual general meeting of the League on his unanimous re-election
in 1935. Moody was a pacifist and supported the Peace Pledge
Union.[21] He was also very wrong in his view that Japan had peaceful
plans for East Asia and the Pacific. (See also pp. 120, 133, 144.)

The objective of the League is, as it has been since its inception, to unite the various elements of our race and kind for the advance of humanity and ourselves. As a Christian, I take my stand on the teaching of Jesus Christ and willingly lend a part of my life and work to the League in this fight to serve in accordance with His standards of goodwill and morality. Present happenings in neurotic Europe point to a redisturbance of Peace on Earth by another war. What is to be the attitude of Negroes throughout the world to this new conflict?

Since the white man chooses to engage in inter-tribal warfare along highly scientific and diabolically efficient lines and to accelerate his decadence thereby, why should we share his ruin? ... I would therefore call upon Africans throughout the world to decide that if Europe chooses to fight, we will on no account take up arms.[22] United response to this call will mean that the 200,000,000 Africans in the world will save Europe, the world and humanity from the bloodiest disaster ever known. Africa will not get her rights unless she is prepared to fight for them. But she must fight in the right way ...

As a race we have in modern times not done anything unitedly and on a really big scale. I feel the time has now come for such action. There are enough capable, honest and racially conscious Africans in the world to carry out this task, big as it, is, quite successfully. We are too apt to suffer from the inferiority complex and to believe that the job is too big for us. I hope the man of tried ability, sane outlook and self-sacrificing disposition throughout the world will respond to this call and join with me to provide the ways and means and carry out the work for the emancipation of our race and humanity at large. Europe will never give this world peace. Africa and Africans can save the world of our day and generation ... Africans Arise!

Source: *The Keys*, 2.4 (April–June 1935), pp. 66–67, 83.

LEARIE CONSTANTINE 1901–71:
Christians and the colour bar in the 1950s

Learie Constantine was born on the West Indian island of Trinidad and brought up as a Roman Catholic. He left school and worked as a clerk until 1927, the year he got married. Constantine's father was a good cricketer and Learie became an excellent fielder. He played for Trinidad and was selected for the West Indian team to tour

England in 1923, and again in 1928 when his skills as bowler, fielder, and scorer helped his side defeat the English team by three wickets. Constantine remained in Britain, playing professional cricket for Nelson in Lancashire, where he and his wife lived until 1949. In Trinidad and in Britain, Constantine experienced racial prejudice; on one occasion he and his wife were turned away from a London hotel although they had booked. Constantine successfully sued the hotel.

Deeply concerned about racial prejudice, he recounts his sad experience of the 'colour bar' among Christians. Constantine was knighted in 1962 and was made a peer in 1969, being the first person of African descent to enter the House of Lords.

> The fact is simple enough. But anyone who knows anything of Africa, or for that matter of the West Indies or even England or the U.S.A., knows perfectly well that the black man is *not*, in general, accepted as fit to take part in religious ceremony together with white worshippers without discrimination. Put it this way. In your church, would you and everyone else make no sign of difference if you found a score of coloured people of all social classes sprinkled about sitting in the church when you arrived? If you are a member of the Church of England, would you and all your fellow church-goers kneel in physical contact with such coloured people at the altar for Communion? Would you have your baby christened in the arms of a Negro priest or your mother buried by one? Would you permit a coloured pastor to kiss your bride, as white pastors sometimes do?
>
> I have had some of the most painful experiences of colour segregation that I have ever suffered in churches in America, the West Indies and England ... I used to be Roman Catholic. Perhaps I could say I am one still, for my belief in God and in the perfect love of Jesus has never wavered. But I have ceased to practise my religion formally. I do not make confession or attend Mass any more, and if I felt I were dying, I do not think I should send for a priest to give me absolution; I would take my chance of God's forgiveness. This is a dreadful thing for a sincere Roman Catholic to say, but I say it because I have suffered so much, and seen my coloured friends suffer so much, at white priests' and white Roman Catholic worshippers' hands ...

Source: Learie Constantine, *Colour Bar* (London, 1954), pp. 108–109.

Notes

1. Cugoana makes up this 'quotation' but it is firmly based on the Bible and includes part of Acts 17:26.

2. Essentially the two great commandments in Matthew 22:37, 39.

3. Henry Thornton, 1760–1820, wealthy evangelical Anglican philanthropist, and member of the anti-slave-trade group known as the 'the Saints' or the 'Clapham Sect'.

4. Thomas Clarkson, 1760–1846, anti-slavery agitator who led the extra-parliamentary campaign against the slave trade. Clarkson's efforts helped to abolish the slave trade in 1807 and to emancipate slaves throughout the British Empire by 1838.

5. Granville Sharp, 1734–1813, anti-slavery activist who successfully brought the Somerset case before Lord Mansfield in 1772.

6. William Wilberforce, 1759–1833, Tory MP, evangelical and leader of the parliamentary opposition to the slave trade. He later campaigned to end slavery in the British Empire.

7. Edward Barrett took his name from the absentee owner of the Oxford estate in northern Jamaica where he was a slave (Edward Moulton Barrett was the father of Elizabeth Barrett Browning). Edward Barrett was freed and became bookkeeper to the estate, with an income of £50 a year in 1838.

8. Revd William Knibb, 1803–45, Baptist missionary in Jamaica who campaigned against slavery.

9. The speeches were reported, but not verbatim, in the BFASS journal, the *Anti-Slavery Reporter*, 20 May 1840, pp. 105–106.

10. 'The Crescent' – the Ottoman Empire.

11. Acts 17:26 in the Authorized Version.

12. 'Ethiopian', a term often used of Africans.

13. That is, the British Empire.

14. Scholes referred to white people as 'the colourless race'.

15. See Acts 17:22.

16. This idea that European learning and culture derived from Africa enjoyed considerable currency in the late twentieth century, largely due to the writings of Martin Bernal, *Black Athena*, 1, 2 (London, 1985, 1991). See Stephen Howe, *Afrocentricism: Mythical Pasts and Imagined Homes* (London, 1998).

17. The campaign for women's suffrage – the right to vote in national

elections – began to gather ground in 1897, although the vote was not gained, for women aged thirty years and over, until 1918.

18. The SANNC, later the African National Congress, was founded in 1912.

19. The Union of South Africa was created by the British Parliament in 1909. The Union Parliament was elected by mainly white men, except in the Cape, and all members were white.

20. Franchise: the right to vote.

21. The Peace Pledge Union was a pacifist and anti-war organization formed by the Revd Dick Shepherd in 1934.

22. During the First World War all the European colonial powers used African troops in the African military campaigns; the French employed West African soldiers in Europe.

4. EVANGELISM AND MISSION

PHILLIS WHEATLEY: A missionary proposal
The idea that former black slaves, and also Africans brought to
Europe for formal education, might return to Africa as missionaries
gained ground on both sides of the Atlantic in the late eighteenth
century. The London merchant and evangelical John Thornton,[1] in
1774, urged Phillis Wheatley to go to West Africa as a missionary
with two Africans who had been brought to Britain for training.
Phillis Wheatley provides a witty but measured reply as to why she
should not be directed in this way. (See also pp. 41, 74.)

> You propose my returning to Africa with Bristol Yamma and John
> Quamine if either of them upon Strict enquiry is Such, as I dare give my
> heart and hand to, I believe they are either of them good enough if not
> too good for me, or they would not be fit for missionaries; but why do
> you hon'd Sir, wish those poor men so much trouble as to carry me So
> long a voyage? Upon my arrival, how like a Barbarian Should I look to
> the Natives; I can promise that my tongue shall be quiet for a strong
> reason indeed being an utter stranger to the Language of Anamaboe.
> Now to be Serious, this undertaking appears too hazardous, and not

sufficiently Eligible, to go – and leave my British & American Friends –
I also unacquainted with those Missionaries in Person. The reverend
gentleman who unde[r] [ta]kes their Education has repeatedly informed
me by Letters of their pro[gress] in Learning and also an Account of
John Quamine's family and Kingdo[m.] But be that as it will I resign it
all to God's all wise governance; I thank you heartily for your generous
Offer – With sincerity –
I am hond. Sir
Most gratefully your devoted Servt.
Phillis Wheatley
Boston October 30th 1770 [1774].

Source: Vincent Carretta, ed., *Phillis Wheatley: Complete Writings* (London,
2001), pp. 159–160.

SAMUEL BARBER:
Urges his mother and sister to trust in Jesus
Samuel Barber, a Primitive Methodist preacher, wrote letters to his
mother and his sister Ann urging them to become Christians. The
letters have not survived but are quoted in his obituary. Barber's
language draws largely on the Authorized Version of the Bible. It
has the insistent tone and content that were widely used by
evangelical Christians in the late eighteenth and early nineteenth
centuries. Today it sounds not only heavy but also too direct and
pointed. It was intended to be so, as a way of bringing non-
Christians to a sense of the consequences of ignoring the claims of
Jesus Christ. It stressed sudden death because it was an age when
a long life was far less certain and most people had personal
knowledge of death. Barber's appeal to his mother and his sister
Ann appears to have been successful. Ann came to live with Samuel
and his family in Tunstall. (See also p. 48.)

To his mother:
Having obtained help, it is for me to be faithful, and more especially as
the eternal interest of an affectionate mother is at stake; and shall I be
silent while I see the wolf of hell, leading down to his infernal region, she
who bore me? God forbid! I entreat, beseech you dear mother, deceive
not your mortal soul; obey the request of your maker; 'Wash you, make

you clean,' – 'And I will turn my hand upon thee, and purely purge
away thy dross, and take away all thy tin.'

To his sister Ann:
Dear Sister ... redeem the time, escape for thy life, seek for mercy
while it may be found. Time is short, eternity is at hand ... Oh, my
dear sister ... My soul longs for you. I would snatch you as a brand
from the burning; awake thou that sleepeth, and Christ shall give
you light.

Source: 'Memoir of Samuel Barber, a local preacher', by John
Smith, *The Primitive Methodist Magazine for the Year 1829*, 10,
pp. 119–121.

JOSEPH JACKSON FULLER 1825–1908:
Missionary patience

Joseph Jackson Fuller was born a slave in Jamaica. In 1844, with his
father Alexander, he was among the first Jamaican missionaries to
go to work on the West African island of Fernando Po. Later he
moved to Cameroon and undertook Bible translating work. Fuller's
first wife and several of his children died in Africa. Relations
between black and white missionaries were not always easy, as
Fuller indicates in this extract from his unpublished autobiography.
(See also p. 112.)

Differences had now grown to such a pitch between the brethren that
some of the men proposed to me to cut my connection with the Society
[Baptist Missionary Society] and that they had friends enough in England
that would enable us to carry on our work in Africa; but I could not see
it desirable to do so, and at the same time I had never been to England
so knew nothing personally of the Society nor of friends. I had been
through much with native savages and God has helped me, and why
should I take notice of minor troubles, so I declined to have anything to
do with the dissatisfactions going on, I did my work and left things to
right themselves ...

Source: BMS Archives, Angus Library, Oxford. A/5/19. 'Autobiography
of the Rev. J. J. Fuller of Cameroons, West Africa'.

JOSEPH JACKSON FULLER:
Addressing the Baptist Union, Cambridge

Fuller first visited England in 1869, accompanied by his second wife
Charlotte, whom he had married in 1861, and their two sons. Fuller
was invited to attend the Baptist autumnal meetings in Cambridge
and to his great surprise he was asked to speak. In the early 1880s
the Fullers retired to live in England. They were members of Stoke
Newington Baptist Church and Fuller spoke at Christian meetings
around Britain.

In the evening there was a public meeting and ... so I secreted myself in
one corner of the great hall which was very large and crowded to its
utmost, when a gentleman came up and [said] ... 'You are wanted.'
I followed him ... [and] to my surprise I was invited on to the platform.

[The] President of the union gave a short detailed account of my
father's visit to England[2] on his way to Africa and of the pleasure he had
in hearing him, then turning to me, he said, 'I now have the pleasure of
seeing his son, who has been a missionary in Africa, and we shall be glad
of a few words from him.' How I felt then I can scarcely describe, except
to say that if I could have slipped down some hole and disappeared I
should have been glad to have done so but there was no means of doing
so, I had then to face the difficulty, God helping me, for I had never
spoken to such an assembly in my life and for so many years speaking
the African language, I felt how incapable I was to speak to such an
audience in English and in such a city.

What I said was very kindly received and from what followed I
believed appreciated for from that day I was marked for deputation work
all over the country and so great was the demand for my services that I
could not go to all the places but wherever I went I was very kindly
received and the meetings encouraging...

Source: BMS Archives, Angus Library, Oxford. A/5/19. 'Autobiography
of the Rev. J. J. Fuller of Cameroons, West Africa'.
See further: Jeffrey Green, 'Joseph Jackson Fuller', in Colin Matthew and
John Harrison, eds., *Oxford Dictionary of National Biography* (Oxford, 2004),
21, pp. 150–151; Las Newman, 'A West Indian contribution to Christian
mission in Africa: the career of Joseph Jackson Fuller (1845–1888)', in
Transformation 18.4 (2001), pp. 220–231.

THOMAS L. JOHNSON 1836–1921: Death of his wife

Thomas L. Johnson was born into slavery in Virginia. He gained his freedom at the end of the American Civil War in 1865. Johnson's ambition was to go to Africa as a missionary. To secure a better education he came to Britain and studied at The Pastor's College[3] in London (1876–78). In 1878 he and his fellow black student, Calvin Richardson, with their wives (they were sisters), sailed to Cameroon in West Africa to work for the Baptist Missionary Society. They travelled inland to the station at Bakunda. It was a difficult and painful time for Johnson. Both Johnson and his wife Henrietta were ill and in late 1879 Henrietta died of fever. In a letter to C. H. Spurgeon,[4] Johnson described his wife's death but his continuing faith in God. (See also pp. 64, 114, 118.)

Abut six weeks before her death she was much better, and the fevers all left her ... On the following Wednesday afternoon I said: "Henrietta, do you love Jesus?" Her lips moved, but she was too helpless to lift her hands. Just before candlelight I asked her if I should read the Bible. Her lips again moved, so I read part of John xiv. At eight o'clock she commenced to breathe hard, and looked at me as though she wanted to speak. This lasted just a minute or two, and then she went home to live with my blessed Jesus. She is indeed now at rest and free. Since the death of my dear wife I thought at one time I should soon follow her. My heart seemed to be affected in some way, and I suffered also from fever and neuralgia; but God has seen fit to raise me up again. I am much better, but far from being well. I wish sometimes I could come home and stay for five or six months. I sometimes fear that I shall not be able to do the good I had hoped to do in Africa, but my Father knows all about it. If He wants me to serve Him in this way, Amen, *God's way is always the best way*... Please ask the friends at the prayer meeting to pray for the success of our work at Bakundu. I am praying for the conversion of the young king.

Yours truly, for Africa,

Thomas L. Johnson

Source: *The Sword and Trowel* (January 1880), p. 43. Thomas L. Johnson, *Twenty-Eight Years a Slave, or the Story of My Life in Three Continents* (Bournemouth, 7th edn, 1909), p. 137.

THOMAS L. JOHNSON: An uncomfortable African journey
Johnson fell sick working as a missionary in Cameroon and he had
to return to Britain. Here he describes an incident on his journey,
carried in a hammock, to the coast.

As we left the village we had to cross a small stream, though quite deep.
The trunk of a large tree, which had fallen across the water, formed a
bridge. A long vine of some kind ... was stretched across as a support for
one crossing over. I was carried over on the back of a native. Mr. Wilson
[African pastor] went ahead. The man who carried me was trusting greatly
to this vine to support himself. When we were half way across the son of
the Chief appeared at the other end of the bridge and ordered us to go
back. This Mr. Wilson refused to do. He then threatened to cut the vine
loose if we did not go back. The current of the stream at this spot was
very strong, and as I looked at the water, my head began to 'swim.'
Mr. Wilson then said, 'Look up, Mr. Johnson.' I did so, and at once
commenced to pray for deliverance, and benefited doubly by the act.
    Mr. Wilson then said to the young man in native language,
'Mr. Johnson had been to see your mother and made a present – "dash." '
And he at once allowed us to cross. It was evidently God's leading in my
going to see his mother and giving her that knife, which had proved to be
keener of edge than I had thought. Again I see in this God's hand.

Source: Thomas L. Johnson, *Twenty-Eight Years a Slave or the Story of My Life
in Three Continents* (Bournemouth, 7th edn, 1909), pp. 138–139.

THEOPHILUS SCHOLES: Arrival in Africa
Dr Theophilus Scholes toured Scotland and Ireland with a fellow
black Christian, Thomas L. Johnson, speaking and raising money in
support of 'The African Mission'. In February 1886, he sailed from
Liverpool to the Congo where, for two years, he ran a sanatorium.
In this letter to Johnson, Scholes described his arrival in the Congo.
(See also p. 95.)

Congo Hotel, March 25th 1886

Dear friend,
I hail this opportunity of writing from this stage of our journey. In

answer to prayer, no doubt, our Heavenly Father brought us hither in safety yesterday morning. You will be curious to know the kind of reception we had after the pictures we had presented as to the manner we should be received owing to our colour. I frankly confess that after taking into consideration the fact that we came without any introduction to the agent of the Dutch House, our reception by gentlemen in connection with that firm, and others whom I have met since arrival, was most courteous. We shall be two days here, as the Dutch House steamer leaves for the river in the forenoon tomorrow (D.V.).[5] I had an interview with Mr. De Bloeme respecting the receiving and forwarding of our goods, etc., henceforth. He has agreed to do it at a premium of ten per cent of mail rates. This, I understand, is a new arrangement which is to apply to all missions alike.

Source: Thomas L. Johnson, *Twenty-Eight Years a Slave or the Story of My Life in Three Continents* (Bournemouth, 7th edn, 1909), p. 178.

SAMUEL JULES CELESTINE EDWARDS 1856–94:
Confronting atheism
Samuel Jules Celestine Edwards came from the West Indian island of Dominica. He went to a Wesleyan school in Antigua, but, eager for adventure, he became a seaman and travelled around the world, arriving in Britain in the late 1870s. He was converted in 1880, joined the Primitive Methodists, and worked as a gospel temperance lecturer and evangelist in the north of England. Edwards spoke and wrote passionately about Christian faith, arguing that this should be demonstrated in the conduct of political and imperial affairs in Africa. He also edited two journals. Suffering from consumption, Edwards returned to Dominica, where he died.

In the face of organised Unbelief, with its three weekly newspapers, its tracts, and lecturers, are we to sit down quietly and let them capture our youths as soon as they leave the Sunday schools? Must we leave the clerks and artisans to their mercy? Ten thousand times, no! Let every Christian gird up his loins, put on the whole armour of God, and never lay down his weapon until his tongue cleaves to the roof of his mouth, and his hand forgets its cunning. We must make sure of the grounds of our belief, and fashion our lives in harmony with Christ, close our ranks

S. J. Celestine Edwards, Bible class leader, evangelist and newspaper editor, smartly dressed in this confident pose, photographed in the 1890s.

and use every legitimate means to build up the faith of our fellowmen; we must tell men why they must believe, and show them the instability of the ground of unbelief. Above all, we must emphasis the fact that Christianity is not afraid of examination, but demands a merciless experiment.

Source: S. J. Celestine Edwards, 'Our Convictions', *Lux*, 1.1 (6 August 1892), p. 1.
See further: Jonathan Schneer, in Colin Matthew and John Harrison, eds., *Oxford Dictionary of National Biography* (Oxford, 2004), 17, pp. 912–913.

GREGORY MPIWA NGCOBO 1876–1931:
Missionary in southern Africa

Gregory Ngcobo grew up at Isandhlwana in Zululand, where he was baptized and confirmed at the local Anglican mission. In 1891, aged fourteen, he was sent to England and studied first in Sussex and then at St Augustine's College, Canterbury, where he undertook a missionary training course. Ngcobo returned home to Zululand late in 1897 to work for the Society for the Propagation of the

Gregory Ngcobo was one of a number of black South Africans who came
to train at St Augustine's College, Canterbury, in the nineteenth century.
In this photograph, taken in 1897, he is seated third from the left. Gregory
returned to southern Africa to teach and to preach.

Gospel, and nine years later he was ordained a priest. Gregory
Ngcobo was killed in a road accident in August 1931. In this letter,
sent to St Augustine's College, he describes the impact of the South
African War (1899–1902) on the school where he worked.

Isandhlwana June 17th 1900

The Boers, after taking the Nqutu Magistracy, came on here. We were
just looking at them passing about a mile away ... when a messenger
came up summoning the head, Mr R. B. Davies of the mission station, to
go and meet their commander. The 3 boys and myself accompanied him.
The Commander only told us how he took the Ngutu and made its
inhabitants prisoners of Pretoria [capital of the South African Republic],
then we all walked back to the College, where they all joined together,
offsaddled, & asked for some fruits, which were then plentiful. Peaches,
apples & Grapes were all served to them in due order: they were 38 of

them. The Commander, who called himself Joubert, addressed the
natives (which were in great number for curiosity than anything) in Zulu
to this import. If anywhere they were to see two lions at fight, & the one
was gradual gaining ground & pushing the other back, what would they
understand of it? & that was the way how they were to understand of
the retreat of the English. They after that were frequently seen riding
about, shooting at the bucks. But besides the looting the stores, and
commandeering horses, they offered no other violence. They took two
horses from this place belonging to a J.P govt. official. This district was
reoccupied by the English last May.

Source: Canterbury Cathedral Archives, Canterbury, Kent. U88 A2/6
C745/12(1).

THOMAS L. JOHNSON:
Preaching and personal evangelism

Thomas L. Johnson, who had trained to be a Baptist minister and
missionary, lived much of his later life in Britain, where he was an
evangelist. His autobiography, first published in 1882, appeared in
seven editions. Johnson was often very direct in talking to people
about 'my dear Jesus'. Here he describes talking to a man on a train
on a journey through Essex in 1894. (See also pp. 64, 113.)

... a man sat in front of me in the railway carriage. He looked very sad.
Something seemed to say to me, – "Speak to that man." At last I asked
him if he knew Jesus. Oh, he had been brought up in a Christian family,
and had attended the Methodist Church nearly all his life-time. "But are
you saved?" I enquired. He confessed that he was not; and then he told
me about his troubles, entering into home affairs which were very sad.
I tried to show him his only path to peace and happiness, which was in
complete surrender to our Lord Jesus Christ; and then I explained to him
the way of salvation, and urged immediate decision. He desired me to
pray for him, and I did; but I told him he must pray for himself. He said
he could not do this. I insisted that it was a personal matter, and that he
must give himself right up; I could got [sic] no further with him. At
length he got on his knees, gave himself to Jesus, and commenced to
pray also for his wife and children and father and mother. He rose from
his knees weeping and happy.

Source: Johnson, *Twenty-Eight Years a Slave or the Story of My Life in Three Continents* (Bournemouth, 7th edn, 1909), pp. 251–252.

J. ALBERT THORNE 1860–1939:
'An appeal addressed to the friends of the African race'

Albert Thorne was born in Barbados. He lived in Britain from 1884 to 1897 and studied medicine at Aberdeen University. Thorne promoted a scheme that would help settle West Indian missionaries in Nyasaland, which was then being brought under British colonial control. Albert Thorne argued that his scheme would help to bring central Africa 'under the influence of Christian men' whom by 'loving contact with their needy brethren' would 'produce the best results'. He explained his vision in a letter to a British newspaper. Little came of Thorne's ambitious idea. He lived much of his later life in New York, where he died and is buried.

> The rapid development of Africa, together with the success of those who have gone thither from England and Scotland ... opened my eyes [to] the immense possibilities of that country. And I reasoned ... surely if the white man can do all this in a country where the climate is against them and ... the prejudice of the native races ... enterprising and well trained Africans should be able to do it also. Therefore ... I conceived the plan of African colonization with which my name is now connected.

Source: *York Gazette*, 1 August 1899.
See further: Robert A. Hill, 'Zion on the Zambesi: Dr J. Albert Thorne, "A Descendant of Africa and Barbados", and the African colonial enterprise: The "preliminary stage", 1894–7', in Jagdish G. Sundara and Ian Duffield, eds., *Essays on the History of Blacks in Britain* (Aldershot, 1992), pp. 99–123.

SALIM WILSON: Dispute on the mission field

Salim Wilson went as a missionary to the Congo and then to North Africa. Salim's missionary activity in the Congo was brief. The plan of the missionary Graham Wilmot Brooke[6] was to enter Sudan via the Congo. With his knowledge of Sudanese Arabic and smattering of other local languages, Salim was enlisted by Brooke for this venture. Things did not go well. Brooke probably thought himself superior to his black companion and treated him more as a servant than as a companion. Within a year the two men parted company and Salim returned to Britain. Below is Salim's account of the mission's failure. After missionary work in North Africa, Salim spent most of his life in England, where he gained a reputation as the 'black evangelist of the north'. He was buried alongside his white wife in Scunthorpe. (See also p. 67.)

> Mr. Brooke had been for some time gradually changing his Theological views, and we were no longer able to see eye to eye in matters of doctrine. Nor could we agree in our ideas as to what ought to be done when we found ourselves unable to get into the Soudan ... Had it been possible for us to reach my own People, I should have gone at any risk. It would have been the joy of joys to me to have declared the Word of Life to the Dinka, the Niamin [Azande], or the Bongo Peoples; but I knew nothing of the languages of the Peoples whose countries Mr. Brooke wished to penetrate. Thus we were compelled to part. At the time it was the greatest trial that could have fallen upon me. It sorely tried my faith and was a bitter disappointment to my long-cherished hopes of preaching the Gospel in my native country. It was a struggle of heart to be resigned to the will of God.

> Source: *Jehovah-Nissi: The Life Story of Hatashil-Masha-Kathish of the Dinka Tribe of the Soudan* (Birmingham, 2nd edn, 1901), p. 73.
> See further: Salim Wilson, *I Was a Slave* (London, n.d., c. 1939); Douglas H. Johnson, 'Salim Wilson: the Black evangelist of the North', *Journal of Religion in Africa* 31.1 (1991), pp. 26–41.

HAROLD MOODY: Missionary endeavour 1931

Dr Harold Moody, a medical doctor with a practice in South London, is best known as the president of the League of Coloured Peoples, founded in 1931 (see p. 104). But he was also an active Christian, deacon of a Congregational church, a lay preacher, and a leading member of the London Missionary Society. When he became president of the London confederation of the Christian Endeavour Union[7] in 1931, he set out his plans to promote the work of mission. (See also pp. 121, 133, 144.)

My idea is that Christian Endeavour should make a larger contribution to the Church life of London on its missionary side ... The slogan we have accepted is 'Youth for Christ and the World.' Following upon the great evangelistic campaign now concluding, where youth has been garnered in to the Kingdom, there ought to be a great impetus in the direction of missionary endeavour. After salvation comes service. We have fixed up a meeting in each of our unions. The line provisionally adopted is that the missionary committee will send out a questionnaire for answer by the churches, revealing what they have done and are doing, their contributions, their contacts with the field and so on ... The chief aim is to increase the missionary interest of the churches and to get lives consecrated for service in the mission field.

Source: *The Christian Endeavour Times* (2 April 1931), p. 527.

HAROLD MOODY: Encouraging disciples 1932

Moody told large Christian Endeavour gatherings in London in 1931–32 that 'the Church is essentially a missionary organization'. In mid-1932, sixty young people met at the Moodys' home in Peckham to dedicate themselves to missionary work. This is what Moody told them. (See also pp. 104, 133, 144.)

Our recruits must be ... prepared to dare everything and to do everything for the sake of the Kingdom of God. In the first place, they must, spare no pains in securing their training ... as Moffatt[8] puts it, 'Do your utmost to let God see that you at least are a sound workman with no need to be ashamed of the way you handle the Word of the Truth.'[9] ... In the second place you must be prepared to 'endure hardness as a good soldier of Jesus Christ.'[10] This is no soft job ... You must be prepared for every eventuality, if necessary, and even to 'rejoice that you were counted worthy to suffer shame for His name.' ...

You must be able to live with your own fellow missionaries in lonely conditions, and you must be able to live with the people among whom you are working ... You cannot go if you are unable to enter into the life and spirit of a people other than your own and to gain their confidence. I have seen missionaries who associate with very questionable persons, simply because they are of their own race ... The modern missionary lives between two fires. It is becoming increasingly difficult today to pursue the life and work of a missionary without being misunderstood either by the people whom you go to help or by your own people. It is fast becoming increasingly necessary for the missionary who is out to do his best by the people whom he goes forth to serve, that he should know something about anthropology – the science of man ... This brings me to my third point. We must be consecrated ... I want you to feel that indeed you are Christ's own, body, soul and spirit, and that while you are doing the utmost yourself, you are dependent upon Him for everything.

Source: Harold A. Moody, 'Contemptible, Compatible, Consecrated: An Address to Missionary Recruits', *The Christian Endeavour Times*, 4 August 1932, p. 115.

CONSTANCE MIREMBE:
A London City Missioner from Africa 2005

The London City Mission was founded in 1835. For most of its history the missioners, working in some of the poorest parts of London, were white men. By the twenty-first century there were black missioners, including women such as Constance Mirembe from Uganda, who, in 2005, was working in Vauxhall. Here she writes about the family influences that helped to shape her life as a missionary in Britain.

I grew up in Uganda in homes (first my parents, then my uncle and auntie's) which were always open to many visitors. Visitors from all walks of life came without notice, twenty-four hours a day and stayed for as long as they wanted, for a day to a month. We grew up watching our parents loving the visitors of the moment as if they were the only ones of the year.

One of my father's teachings was, 'Children: watch how we treat visitors and do likewise. Greet them happily, answer them respectfully, and remember: God took time to create them, he cares for them and watches how we treat them. Above all just love people.'

I didn't know that God was preparing me for today, but my upbringing makes evangelism a meaningful and beautiful job for me. Nothing, nothing at all, would stop me from loving people.

Working in a community such as Vauxhall, one has to keep an open heart and mind. This area accommodates people from all walks of life:

Constance Mirembe, an African missionary in Britain. Constance was born in Uganda but now works for the London City Mission.

it's a big job getting to know them and learning something of their culture. My contacts know that I care, respect and love them fully. It has been possible for them, therefore, wherever they are from, to come to me and know that I'm available for them.

Source: *Changing London*, the magazine of the London City Mission (Winter 2005), p. 16.

_____

Notes

1. John Thornton, 1720–90, a merchant, philanthropist and leading evangelical.
2. Alexander Fuller came from Jamaica to Fernando Po in 1843.
3. See above, p. 72, note 8.
4. Charles Haddon Spurgeon, 1834–92, Baptist preacher and leader.
5. D.V.: *Deo volente*, Latin for 'God being willing'.

6. Graham Wilmot Brooke, 1865–92, independent missionary in Africa, who then joined the CMS in Nigeria, where his 'intense and intolerant spiritual enthusiasm' alienated some of his colleagues and antagonized African clergy; he died of fever.

7. Christian Endeavour Societies, to promote the spiritual life of young people, were founded in Congregational churches in the United States in 1881, with the motto 'For Christ and the Church'. The movement became international and interdenominational and a World Union was created in 1895.

8. James Moffatt, 1870–1944, Church of Scotland minister and academic, who produced a well-known modern translation of the Bible in the years 1913–27.

9. 2 Timothy 2:15.

10. 2 Timothy 2:3.

5. SERVING THE COMMUNITY

IGNATIUS SANCHO: Thoughts on eternity
Ignatius Sancho set up business as a grocer in Charles Street, West-minster. He was widely read, and wrote music and also numerous letters to friends and acquaintances, in some of which he pondered on heaven. After Sancho's death his letters were edited and published in 1782; a fifth edition appeared in 1803. (See also pp. 75, 141.)

... the promise of never, never-ending existence and felicity – to possess eternity – 'glorious dreadful thought!' – to rise, perhaps by regular progression from planet to planet – to behold the wonders of immensity – to pass from good to better – increasing in goodness – knowledge – love – to glory in our Redeemer – to joy in ourselves – to be acquainted with prophets, sages, heroes, and poets of old times – to join in symphony with angels!

Source: Ignatius Sancho, *Letters of the Late Ignatius Sancho, An African* (London, 1782; 5th edn, 1803), Letter XLV, p. 92.
See further: *Letters of the Late Ignatius Sancho,* ed. Paul Edwards (London, 1968).

DAVID GEORGE 1743–1810: A Christian memoir

David George was a slave in the British North American colony of Virginia. He escaped and lived among Native Americans, but was then sold back into slavery in South Carolina. George was converted after hearing a sermon by the black preacher George Liele. During the American war of revolution many slaves, including David George, fled to the British forces. At the end of the war, along with other loyalists, he moved to Nova Scotia, where he pastored a number of Baptist churches. In 1792 George emigrated to the recently created settlement of Freetown on the West African coast. He made a short visit to England, where he dictated his memoirs to the Baptist ministers John Rippon[1] and Samuel Pearce.[2]

[In Nova Scotia] I got leave to go to Shelburne ... Numbers of my own color were here, but I found the White people were against me. I began to sing the first night, in the woods, at a camp, for there were no houses then built; they were just clearing and preparing to erect a town. The Black people came far and near, it was so new to them: I kept on so every night in the week, and appointed a meeting for the first Lord's-day, in a valley between two hills, close by the river; and a great number of White and Black people came, and I was so overjoyed with having an opportunity once more of preaching the word of God, that after I had given out the hymn, I could not speak for tears. In the afternoon we met again, in the same place, and I had great liberty from the Lord. We had a meeting now every evening, and those poor creatures who had never heard the gospel before, listened to me very attentively: but the White people, the justices, and all, were in an uproar, and said that I might go out into the woods, for I should not stay there. I ought to except one White man, who knew me at Savannah, and who said I should have his lot to live upon as long as I would, and build a house if I pleased. I then cut down poles, stripped bark, and made a smart hut, and the people came flocking to the preaching every evening for a month, as though they had come for their supper.

Source: 'An Account of the Life of Mr. DAVID GEORGE from Sierra Leone in Africa; given by himself in a Conversation with Brother

RIPPON of London, and Brother PEARCE of Birmingham', in John Rippon, ed., *The Baptist Annual Register* (1792), pp. 473–483.

See further: Grant Gordon, *From Slavery to Freedom: The Life of David George, Pioneer Black Baptist Minister* (Nova Scotia, 1992); Lamin Sanneh, 'David George', in Gerald H. Anderson, ed., *Biographical Dictionary of Christian Missions* (New York, 1998), pp. 238–239.

BOSTON KING c. 1760–1802: My life

Boston King was born into slavery in South Carolina. He became a Christian while a slave, but felt fully assured of his salvation only while living in Nova Scotia, where he was a Methodist preacher. King went with the black settlers to Freetown in the early 1790s. He wrote an account of his life while studying at the Methodist school at Kingswood, near Bristol, in 1794–6. Returning to Freetown he continued his preaching ministry to his death.

When I first arrived in England, I considered my great ignorance and inability, and that I was among a wise and judicious people, who were greatly my superiors in knowledge and understanding; these reflections had such an effect upon me, that I formed a resolution never to attempt to preach while I stayed in the country; but the kind importunity of the Preachers and others removed my objections, and I found it profitable to my own soul, to be exercised in inviting sinners to Christ; particularly one Sunday, while I was preaching at Snowsfields Chapel, the Lord blessed me abundantly, and I found a more cordial love to the White People than I had ever experienced before. In the former part of my life I had suffered greatly from the cruelty and injustice of the Whites, which induced me to look upon them, in general, as our enemies: And even after the Lord had manifested his forgiving mercy to me, I still felt at times an uneasy distrust and shyness towards them; but on that day the Lord removed all my prejudices; for which I bless his holy Name.

Kingswood-School, June 4, 1796.

Source: 'Memoirs of the Life of BOSTON KING, a Black Preacher. Written by Himself, during his Residence at Kingswood-School'. *The Methodist Magazine*, 21 (London, 1798), pp. 105, 110, 157–161, 209–213, 262–265.

See further: Christopher Fyfe, ed., *Our Children Free and Happy. Letters from Black Settlers in Africa in the 1790s* (Edinburgh, 1991).

JOSEPH WRIGHT c. 1810–c. 1850s:
'The life of Joseph Wright, a native of Ackoo'

Joseph Wright's original name is unknown. He was an Egba from one of the walled towns in a forested area which is now part of southern Nigeria. In his 'Narrative', written in his own hand in April 1839, he says, 'I was born a heathen in a heathen land'. During a war of the 1820s he was sold into slavery, then passed through different African hands and eventually sold to a Portuguese slave trader in Lagos. The slave ship carrying Wright across the Atlantic was seized by a British naval vessel and its cargo of 'recaptives' taken to Freetown. In 1834 he was converted and joined the Methodists. Five years later Wright was a class leader and in the early 1840s he was sent to England for two years training by the Wesleyan Methodist Missionary Society. He returned to Freetown as a native assistant missionary, being ordained in 1848. As Wright makes clear in his 'Narrative', the opportunity to go to school and to learn to read played a vital part in his coming to know Jesus Christ as his Saviour.

> After we were landed at Freetown ... we were placed at school ...
> We began at once to learn to read English books, which books I have cause to praise God of, while I have life and breath; for through the reading of these books I came to know that high and glorious name of Jesus Christ the Saviour. I have to acknowledge that although I read these books which teach me to know Jesus Christ the Saviour, I did not believe in him as I ought to have believed.
>
> In five or six years after I came to this country, I began to learn to pray morning and even; although I did it not from the heart; for I did not know the nature of prayer at the time. In the year 1834 ... I began to attend Methodist Chapel ... When I joined with them, I begin to seek the Lord; and from the time I obtained peace of God, I go among my friends, telling them that the Lord is good; inviting them to come and taste for themselves how good the Lord is ... I find the work of God to be good work, and it hath been the delight of my soul.

Source: John Beecham, *Ashantee and the Gold Coast* (London, 1841),
pp. 357–358.
See further: Philip Curtin, ed., *Africa Remembered: Narratives by West Africans
from the Era of the Slave Trade* (Madison, WI, 1968), pp. 317–333.

JOHN OCANSEY: Britain's Christian heritage 1881

Small communities of formally educated Africans lived in the
coastal towns of West Africa in the nineteenth century. Most were
active Christians and a good many visited Britain to study, for work,
business and pleasure, and sometimes to settle. John E. Ocansey,
from Addah (Ada) in the Gold Coast, was a former slave bought by
the Ocansey family, whose daughter he married. In 1881 Ocansey
visited Liverpool to deal with a lawsuit on behalf of the family. This
was his first trip to a modern industrial country. As a Christian he
saw Britain's economic progress as a result of its Christian heritage,
something which he hoped for Africa.

I consider the distance from Liverpool to London to be equal in
length as from Addah to Cape Coast Castle, and that journey by land
takes us fourteen days, and now I have travelled it in four hours and
a half!

Oh, I do pray that I may live to see one of these railways on the
West Coast of Africa! What a saving of time and trouble it will to the
poor Africans who have to make their long and weary journeys on foot,
carrying their heavy loads on their heads, under a broiling, burning sun!
Oh! May God look down in mercy and remember for good the poor
Africans, that they also may enjoy the benefits, advantages, and pleasures
of knowledge and civilization! Oh! That they would consider and be
wise, and rise up like the prodigal son, and say, 'I will arise and go to my
Father, and will say unto him, Father, I have sinned against heaven and
before thee, and am no more worthy to be called thy son; make me as
one of thy hired servants.'[3] And God, our merciful Father, will in no
wise cast us out; but He will, instead of servants, make us as His dear
children. I have had conversations with many intelligent, high-minded
Christian people in England, and they all say that the improvement of
the white man is derived from nothing but the Word of God. Africa,
I hope, will not cast away this most sacred, precious Word, which is now
being preached amongst them in many places by white men. In some

places it has been preached for fifty years, in others forty, thirty, twenty, and ten years, and in all it has produced some precious fruit. Oh! May the knowledge of the Lord spread over Africa as the waters cover the great deep! Then shall Africa find out her great wealth and riches, – then will the earth yield her increase, and God, even our God, shall bless us.

Source: John E. Ocansey, *African Trading; or the Trials of William Narh Ocansey* (Liverpool, 1881; new edn ed. by Kwame Arhin, Accra, 1989), pp. 37–38.

A. B. C. MERRIMAN-LABOR: Christian England?

Augustus Boyle Chamberlayne Merriman-Labor came to Britain to study law and also to write in 1904. He worked as a clerk and was a Sunday school teacher in the Railway Orphanage in south London. Merriman-Labor was in Britain in 1913 but his movements after that are not known. His book, published in London in 1909, sought to dispel the inflated and romantic ideas that his fellow Creoles[4] had of Britain. He commented on British racial attitudes and ideas, racial discrimination, and the distorted reporting about Africa and Africans in the British press. As a devout Methodist he was surprised to find that Britain was not a 'Christian' country. (See also pp. 98–100.)

I remember worshipping there [St Paul's Cathedral in London] the first Sunday morning of my arrival in England more than five years ago. I saw then, therein, some people promenading arm in arm. Others merely went there to view the monuments and paintings which abound within. A few persons had sketching-books, and a number took their hand-cameras with them ... As regard the worshippers, few joined in the prayers, and fewer still answered 'Amen.' The choir for the most part sang alone...

My impression that first Sunday in London was far from being favourable, especially as I noticed, on my way home, that the observance of the Sabbath was different from the mode which prevails in Christianised West Africa. I found so many shops and drinking saloons open. Newspapers were being sold everywhere. Railway and cycling excursions were frequent. Trams and other vehicles went up and down as on week-days.

Sierra Leoneans in London, 1921. London was an Imperial crossroads where all sorts of people from all parts of the British Empire might meet. This photograph, taken in North London in 1921, shows a gathering of eminent Sierra Leoneans at the home of J. Eldred Taylor, a businessman and newspaper proprietor. Several of the people shown here were active Christians.

> I reached home to find that no one at my residence, other than myself, went to service. In fact when I returned from church, my landlady and her daughters ridiculed me for having gone ... She laughed me to scorn when I suggested that herself, myself, and her other lodgers should be holding family prayers.

Source: A. B. C. Merriman-Labor, *Britons Through Negro Spectacles* (London, 1909), pp. 72–74.

JAMES EMMAN KWEGYIR AGGREY 1875–1927:
'Africa the first Christian continent'

Aggrey was born at Anomabo in the British colony of the Gold Coast in October 1875. He was educated in local Methodist schools and became a teacher. In 1898 Aggrey went to study at Livingstone College[5] in the United States, and he was ordained in the African Methodist Episcopal Zion Church. He remained in the United

(Photo by Albert Dennis)

J. E. Kwegyir Aggrey

J. E. Kwegyir Aggrey was a distinguished educationalist. He was born in West Africa in the late nineteenth century but was proud to travel on a British passport.

States as a pastor. Aggrey gained a reputation as a leading educationalist, and this resulted in his appointment to the Phelps-Stokes Fund Commission,[6] which toured Africa to look at educational provision for Africans. He became assistant principal of the newly founded Achimota College, in the Gold Coast, in the 1920s. Aggrey made several visits to Britain. In September 1924 he spoke at a conference on Africa held at High Leigh in Hertfordshire. In the audience was Edwin Smith.[7] 'If I had known then', wrote Smith, 'that I was to write his biography I should have made full notes of what he said. I remember his rather diffident demeanour, his ready wit, his sound sense, but I have only fragmentary records of his words, such as follow.'

> The natives of Africa are awake: the question is, will our guardians
> measure up to our expectations?... We Africans do not know the

difference between religion and business ... Eliminate by substitution ... If you cut us, we get excited ... Strengthen the hereditary chiefs. We don't want education that does not produce character ... The Christian man who comes among us must be one of us ... It is only Christians who meet together like this to criticise themselves to see how they can serve us better ... No first-class educated African wants to be a white man ... Every educated Negro wants to be a first-class Negro, not a third-class European ... The superiority complex is doing a tremendous lot of mischief in Africa ... When I am worried, I go on my knees and I talk to God in my own tongue ... I plead with the Christian Church to make Africa the first Christian continent. For God's sake give Africa Christian leaders.

Source: Edwin Smith, *Aggrey of Africa* (London, 1929), p. 231.

HAROLD MOODY: Christian lobbyist

Harold Moody came from Jamaica in 1904 to study medicine at London University. He married a white British wife, and set up a medical practice in South London. As a student and as a doctor he encountered racial prejudice. He hoped that the churches and Christian organizations with which he was actively involved would take a leading part in combating what was then referred to as the 'colour bar'. When this failed to happen, Moody, with others, established the League of Coloured Peoples (LCP) in 1931. In 1934 the LCP sent delegates on a fact-finding visit to South Wales to inquire into discrimination against black British seamen by employers and trade unions. At the same time Moody pressured government ministers and officials, Members of Parliament, ship-owners, and trade union leaders to deal with the abuse. The League inquiry in Cardiff also highlighted the social conditions of many of the black people living in that city. (See also pp. 104, 134, 144.)

> The economic condition of our people in Cardiff is simply appalling and it is to be hoped that the Government and City authorities will quite soon apply themselves seriously to this problem and not allow British citizens to live in a Christian country under conditions which must expose them to great temptations. Certain Christian Churches are working in this district of Cardiff where the majority of these people live.

I have tried, so far without avail, to awaken the Christian conscience of our organised religion to tackle this human problem. Here is a big opportunity for rendering practical Christian service ... I am asserting that ... it is an urgent duty of the Christian Church to make a real study of the spiritual, social and economic conditions of the coloured people in this country with a view to providing an effective solution of the problem. If the Church does not hear this call, it will lose a great opportunity for service and for helping to solve this pressing problem of race. The Kingdom of God cannot come on earth until our prayers are more sincere.

Source: Harold Moody, 'The League of Coloured Peoples and the problem of the Coloured colonial seamen in the United Kingdom', *The Keys*, 3.2 (October–December 1935), p. 23.

HAROLD MOODY:
A challenge to young British Christians 1935
Dr Harold Moody was an active Congregationalist and a much-sought-after preacher who spoke all over the country. In 1931 he became London president of the large youth organization Christian Endeavour; four years later he was elected British national president. Here he addresses members of Christian Endeavour, an organization to which he had belonged as a young man in Kingston, Jamaica. (See also p. 144.)

I have set out upon a great 'adventure.' My desire is to help to break down, wherever they exist, those barriers which divide man from man and race from race, and to demonstrate to the world that there is a something which unites man to man far more important and wonderful than anything which divides them ...

It is to this splendid 'adventure' for the sake of 'Christ and His Kingdom' that I would now call you. Any nation which denies the full benefits of civilisation to any section of its people, or allows any section of its people to become degraded, is a nation without vision, and therefore doomed to perish. In the interests of our own nation and of humanity at large we can do no other than venture forth to precipitate this 'vision splendid' into some something living and practical, for nothing alters in this world except someone alters it. For this we shall need hardness and asceticism, courage and consecration, combat and concentration.

Source: ' "Adventure", by HAROLD A. MOODY, MD., B.S. (President-designate of the British C.E. Union). An Address delivered, at Richmond Hill Congregational Church, Bournemouth, Whit-Tuesday Evening, June, 11th, 1935'. *The Christian Endeavour Times*, 27 June 1935, p. 45.

G. DANIELS EKARTE c. 1890s–1964: The African Churches Mission in Liverpool

Pastor G. Daniels Ekarte was a well-known but controversial figure in Liverpool during the 1930s–60s. In the summer of 1930 he established the African Churches Mission in the working-class and multi-ethnic district of Toxteth. The achievement was remarkable in that Ekarte was untrained and not very well educated, and had arrived without money in the city ten years before. Ekarte ran the Mission as a community centre with Sunday services, a Mothers' Union, Scout and Girl Guide groups, musical activities, and free meals for the poor. He was also concerned with the welfare and working conditions of African seaman. To many black working-class people in Liverpool, Ekarte was a godly man with an open door, a warm heart and a generous pocket. (See also p. 51.)

The African Churches Mission in Liverpool, since its inception in 1931, has been conducted by Rev. G. D. Ekarte. During the past six years, he has done invaluable work among the numerous coloured population in Liverpool, and no one in hunger ever calls on him in vain. His work is fully recognised by the local authorities, who always consult him in case of difficulty with coloured people. The League of Coloured Peoples has decided to develop his work, and to give Mr. Ekarte all the support which lies in its power. In the meanwhile Mr. Ekarte is trying to rejuvenate the branch of the League which was founded in Liverpool some years ago.

Source: *The Keys* 5.1 (July–September 1937), p. 30.
See further: Marika Sherwood, *Pastor Daniels Ekarte and the African Churches Mission* (London, 1994).

PAUL BOATENG (born 1951): Faith in practice

The Rt. Hon. Paul Boateng was MP for Brent South from 1987 to 2005, and, as Chief Secretary to the Treasury from 2002 to 2005, the first black member of the Cabinet. He was appointed as Britain's High Commissioner to South Africa in 2005. Paul Boateng was born in North London of a Ghanaian father and a British mother, at a time when there were relatively few black people living in that area. He trained as a lawyer. Here he talks about his Christian faith in practice.

> Christ challenges us to transform ourselves, and through so doing to transform the world. There is no easy comfort in his love. We have the assurance that he loves us, that we are saved, but at the same time we have a very clear imperative to change, to make ourselves conform more to the very best in us and to Christ's vision for us and for our world. That's the challenge that all Christians face constantly in their lives.
>
> We are fractured, splintered beings, we live in a fractured, splintered world; but through the power of Christ's love we can do better – better ourselves and better in and for the world. I do not believe that politicians face any more challenges in that regard than teachers, than lorry drivers, than shop assistants, than journalists. We are all challenged as Christians and we all have to hope that through prayer, through reflection, through fellowship we are able to maximise the opportunities we have to witness to Christ's love in the world and what it can do.

Source: *Third Way*, April 2004, p. 17.

Notes

1. John Rippon, 1751–1836, evangelical Baptist minister; the *Baptist Annual Register* was the first regular journal for Particular Baptists.
2. Samuel Pearce, 1766–99, Baptist minister and proponent of overseas mission.
3. Luke 15:19.
4. Creoles: the descendants of the black and African peoples who settled in Freetown after 1787.
5. The College, in Salisbury, North Carolina, was organized by the African Methodist Episcopal Zion Church in 1882. It is named after David

Livingstone's son Robert, who died there in a large Confederate prison camp in 1864.

6. See above, p. 72, note 13.

7. Edwin Williams Smith, 1876–1957, Primitive Methodist missionary in southern and central Africa, who became a distinguished anthropologist.

6. CHRISTIAN LIFE

BRITON HAMMON (eighteenth century): British sailor
Hammon was a free black man in the British North American
colony of Massachusetts. In late 1747, with the permission of his
employer, he joined a ship and sailed for the Caribbean. He
experienced many hardships in that region, including shipwreck,
capture by Native Americans, and several years' imprisonment by
the Spanish in Cuba. In 1758 Hammon succeeded in escaping
aboard a British warship. He served in the Royal Navy and saw
action against the French and was wounded. Hammon's *Narrative*
was 'taken down' by a white writer from his oral account. It is the
first known published work in English by a black author. Nothing is
known of Hammon's personal religious faith, although at several
points in his *Narrative* he credits divine providence with his rescue
or escape, and he concludes by praising God for his goodness in
bringing him safely back to the American colonies.

> After being at Jamaica a short Time we sail'd for *London*, as convoy to a
> Fleet of Merchantmen, who all arrived safe in the *Downs*,[1] I was turned
> over to another Ship, the *Arcenceil*, and there remained about a Month.

From this Ship I went on board the *Sandwich* of 90 Guns; on board the *Sandwich*, I tarry'd 6 Weeks, and then was order'd on board the *Hercules*, Capt. *John Porter*, a 74 Gun Ship, we sail'd on a Cruize, and met with a *French* 84 Gun Ship, and had a very smart Engagement, in which about 70 of our Hands were Kill'd and wounded, the Captain lost his Leg in the Engagement, and I was Wounded in the Head by a small Shot. We should have taken this Ship, if they had not cut away the most of our Rigging; however, in about three Hours after, a 64 Gun Ship, came up with and took her – I was discharged from the Hercules the 12th Day of *May* 1759 (having been on board of that Ship 3 Months) on account of my being disabled in the Arm, and render'd incapable of Service, after being honourably paid the Wages due to me. I was put into the *Greenwich* Hospital[2] where I stay'd and soon recovered.

Source: *NARRATIVE of the UNCOMMON SUFFERINGS AND surprizing DELIVERANCE OF BRITON HAMMON, A Negro Man, – Servant to GENERAL WINSLOW, of Marshfield, in NEW-ENGLAND...* (Boston, 1760), pp. 11–12.

JAMES ALBERT UKAWSAW GRONNIOSAW:
A love story

Gronniosaw became a seaman and then enlisted in the army. At some time in the 1760s he arrived at Portsmouth only to be greatly disappointed to find that many Britons were not Christians. He moved to London, where he met George Whitefield,[3] and took lodgings in Petticoat Lane, where he met his future wife Betty, a widow with a young child. His *Narrative* provides one of the earliest love stories by a black Briton. (See also p. 140.)

The morning after I came to my new lodging [in Petticoat Lane], as I was at breakfast with the gentlewoman of the house, I heard the noise of some looms over our heads: I enquir'd what it was; she told me that a person was weaving silk. – I expressed a great desire to see it, and asked if I might: She told me she would go up with me; she was sure I should be very welcome. She was as good as her word, and as soon as we enter'd the room, the person [Betty] that was weaving look'd about, and smiled upon us, and I loved her from that moment. – She ask'd me many questions, and I in return talk'd a great deal to her. I found that she was a member of Mr. Allen's[4] Meeting, and I begun to entertain a good opinion of her, though I was almost afraid to indulge this inclination, least she should prove like all the rest that I had met with at Portsmouth, &c. and which had almost given me a dislike to all white women. – But after a short acquaintance I had the happiness to find she was very different, and quite sincere, and I was not without hope that she entertain'd some esteem for me...

I firmly believed that we should be very happy together, and so it prov'd, for she was given me from the Lord. And I have found her a blessed partner, and we have never repented, tho' we have gone through many troubles and difficulties.

Source: James Albert Ukwsaw Gronniosaw, *A Narrative of the Most Remarkable Particulars in the Life of James Albert Ukawsaw Gronniosaw, An African Prince, as Related by Himself* (Bath, 1772), pp. 35–36, 39.

JAMES ALBERT UKAWSAW GRONNIOSAW:
The misfortunes of the poor

Many black people in eighteenth-century Britain were poor and lived precarious lives. Unemployment was often never far away and this meant that a family might be without money, food and shelter. Under the English Settlement Laws people were entitled to poor relief only in the parish of their birth or if they had lived for several years in another parish. Many black Britons, like Gronniosaw, had not been born in England or Wales, and often they moved about in search of work. In Colchester, Essex, where he had moved with his wife and children, parish help was not available.

...when the winter came on I was discharged ... And now the prospect began to darken upon us again. We thought it most adviseable to move our habitation a little nearer to the Town, as the house we lived in was very cold, and wet, and ready to tumble down...

My dear wife and I were now both unemployed, we could get nothing to do. The winter prov'd remarkably severe, and we were reduc'd to the greatest distress imaginable. – I was always very shy at asking for any thing; I could never beg; neither did I chuse to make known our wants to any person, for fear of offending, as we were entire strangers; but our last bit of bread was gone, and I was obliged to think of something to do for our support. – I did not mind for myself at all; but to see my dear wife and children in want, pierc'd me to the heart...

Gronniosaw and his family moved to Norwich and then to Kidderminster.

Such is our situation at present. – My wife, by hard labor at the loom, does every thing that can be expected from her towards the maintenance of our family; and GOD is pleased to incline his People at times to yield us their charitable assistance; being myself through age and infirmity able to contribute but little to their support. As Pilgrims, and very poor Pilgrims, we are travelling through many difficulties towards our HEAVENLY HOME, and waiting patiently for his gracious call, when the LORD shall deliver us out of the evils of this present world and bring us to the EVERLASTING GLORIES of the world to come. – To HIM be PRAISE for EVER and EVER, AMEN.

Source: James Albert Ukwsaw Gronniosaw, *A Narrative of the Most Remarkable Particulars in the Life of James Albert Ukawsaw Gronniosaw, An African Prince, as Related by Himself* (Bath, 1772), pp. 42–49.

IGNATIUS SANCHO: A letter to a young man in India 1778
Ignatius Sancho lived in Westminster with his black wife and six children: five girls and a boy. He was a man of property and entitled to vote. Sancho wrote many chatty letters to friends, and these were published in 1782, two years after his death. It is clear from some of Sancho's letters that he was a Christian believer. What form his Christianity took we may never know. One of Sancho's letters was to a young man recently gone to India. (See also pp. 75, 125.)

To Mr. J[ack]W[ingrav]E., 1778

I never see your poor father but his eyes betrays his feelings for the hopeful youth in India – A tear of joy dancing upon the lids is a plaudit not to be equalled this side death! – See the effects of right-doing, my worthy friend – Continue in the track of rectitude – and despise poor paltry Europeans – titled, Nabobs – Read your Bible –

As day follows night, God's blessing follows virtue – honor and riches bring up the rear – and the end is peace. – Courage, my boy – I have done preaching.

Source: Ignatius Sancho, *Letters of the Late Ignatius Sancho, An African* (London, 1782, in two volumes; 1803 edn in one volume), Letter LXVIII, p. 147.

JOHN MARRANT 1755–91: Sailor and preacher

Marrant was a free black, born in the British colony of New York. As a teenager he went to one of George Whitefield's evangelistic meetings with the intention of disrupting the service. Instead he was dramatically converted. Marrant had an adventurous life which included capture by Native Americans, and service in the Royal Navy during the American war of independence. In the early 1780s he came to Britain, lived in London, and became a preacher. Marrant was ordained in Bath at Lady Huntingdon's[5] suggestion in 1785. His *Narrative*, published in Bath that year, went into several editions. Marrant went as a missionary to Nova Scotia, married there, and returned to Britain in 1790. He died the following year in London, aged thirty-five, and was buried in Islington.

Some time after this I was cruising about in the American seas, and cannot help mentioning a singular deliverance I had from the most imminent danger, and the use the Lord made of it to me. We were overtaken by a violent storm; I was washed overboard, and thrown on again; dashed into the sea a second time, and tossed upon deck again ... I was in the engagement with the Dutch off the Dogger Bank,[6] on board the Princess Amelia, of eighty-four guns. We had a great number killed and wounded; the deck was running with blood; six men were killed, and three wounded, stationed at the same gun with me; my head and face were covered with the blood and brains of the slain: I was wounded, but did not fall, till a quarter of an hour before the engagement ended, and was happy in my soul during the whole of it.

Source: John Marrant, *A Narrative of the Lord's wonderful dealings with John Marrant, a Black (Now going to preach the Gospel in Nova-Scotia)* (London, 4th edn, 1785), pp. 37–38.

See further: Vincent Carretta, ed., *Unchained Voices: An Anthology of Black Authors in the English-Speaking World of the 18th Century* (Lexington, 1996), pp. 126–127.

GEORGE LIELE c. 1750–1828: A letter of recommendation

Liele, born a slave in Virginia, was the first Baptist missionary to go to a foreign land. He was ordained as a missionary in 1775 to work among black people in the Savannah area of Georgia. Like many slaves he sided with the British during the revolutionary war, along with his master, who freed him in 1778. In 1783 he and his family were evacuated to Jamaica. Liele gained permission to preach to slaves, which unpaid ministry he did while supporting his family by farming. Largely due to his work, Baptist churches were established in Jamaica; by 1814 these had around 8,000 members, mainly slaves. It was customary then for Baptists, when they moved to another place and church, to take with them a letter of recommendation from their minister. This letter from George Liele recommends Hannah Williams, of whom nothing more is known, who came to England in 1791. When printed in the *Baptist Register* it was slightly amended by John Rippon,[7] the editor.

> Kingston, Jamaica. We that are of the Baptist Religion, being separated from all churches, excepting they are of the same faith and order after Jesus Christ, according to the scriptures, do certify, that our beloved *Sister Hannah Williams, during the time she was a member of the church at Savannah, until the evacuation, did walk as* a faithful well-behaved Christian, and do recommend her to join any church of the same faith and order. Given under my hand this 21st day of December, in the year of our Lord, 1791. GEORGE LIELE

Source: John Rippon, *The Baptist Annual Register for 1792* (London, 1793), 1, p. 44.

LOUIS ASA-ASA c. 1810–?: A freed slave in England

Louis Asa-Asa was born somewhere in West Africa. When he was twelve or thirteen years old he was captured by African raiders and enslaved. After a year or more he was sold off the coast to a French ship, the *Pearl*. The ship lost its bearings and, in bad weather, entered the English port of St Ives, Cornwall. Louis was freed following an appeal to a judge in London by George Stephen (1794–1879), a local evangelical and anti-slavery lawyer. As far is as known, Louis remained in England thereafter and worked as a servant to George Stephen.

> I am very happy to be in England, as far as I am very well; – but I have no friend belonging to me, but God, who will take care of me as he had done already. I am very glad I have come to England, to know who God is. I should like much to see my friends again, but I do not now wish to go back to them: for if I go back to my own country, I might be taken as a slave again. I would rather stay here, where I am free, than go back to my country to be sold. I shall stay in England as long as (please God) I shall live. I wish the King of England could know all I have told you. I wish it that he may see how cruelly we are used. We had no king in our country, or he would have stopt [*sic*] it. I think the King of England might stop it, and this is why I wish him to know it all. I have heard say he is good; and if he is, he will stop it if he can. I am well off myself, for I am well taken care of, and have good bed and clothes; but I wish my own people to be as comfortable.

> Source: *The Narrative of Asa-Asa, A captured African. Added to The History of Mary Prince, A West Indian Slave. Related by Herself* (London: 3rd edn, 1831), pp. 43–44.
> See further: *The History of Mary Prince*, ed. Sara Salih (London, 2000).

HAROLD MOODY: Student life in London

As a teenager, Harold Moody became a Christian and an active member of North Street Congregational Church in Kingston, Jamaica, where he was secretary of the local branch of the Christian Endeavour Union. Moody first acquired his preaching skills in small mission chapels near Kingston. In 1904 he came to London to study medicine at Kings College. Like many students he had to look for somewhere to live. (See also pp. 104, 120, 133, 144.)

> I was given several addresses but everyone seemed unable to take me and after hours of wandering I found myself in a top garret in a house in St. Paul's Road, Canonbury, the best I could get just then. Here I

Dr Harold Moody helped to found the League of Coloured Peoples in 1931 and became its first president. In this photograph, taken in March 1934, members of the League are meeting for their annual conference at High Leigh, Hertfordshire. Moody, wearing plus fours, is seated next to his wife Olive.

entrenched myself but I felt so cold and lonely and miserable ... England, the mother country whom I had learnt was bubbling forth with love and charity towards your colonials especially those who come over to study had given me anything but a warm welcome. Accustomed to early rising in Jamaica and on board ship; – a practice which I still continue – I came down soon after 6 am. on my first morning to discover that all was asleep and that I would have to wait for at least three hours more in the cold before I would be regaled with breakfast. After breakfast I sauntered out armed with a map of London to see something of the marvels of the greatest city in the World. Withal I was feeling intensely lonely and not caring wither I went.

Source: Harold Moody, 'My life', ch. 2, 'England', unpublished manuscript.

Many years later, in a wartime broadcast to the West Indies, Moody described arriving at King's College, standing on a balcony and looking down at the assembled students.

> [They] jostled each other in the crowded main hall and quadrangle outside. I was approached by a fellow student who said that he noted I had joined the Medical Faculty as he had done and just wondered if I would come along with him to the Christian Union Squash. Of course I did!

> Source: Harold Moody, 'Calling the West Indies', BBC broadcast, 2–3 January 1944.

Harold Moody was an able and diligent student and won several prizes at King's College. One prize was an interleaved Bible – with plain pages for notes in between each page of text – which Moody used for the rest of his life, and in which he wrote some of his personal thoughts and sermon notes. On the first day of 1910 he wrote:

> God leads may I follow. Whatsoever my hand findeth to do, may I do it with my might. Never *dis*contented ever *un*contented, Do all to the glory of God. Pains are oft the birth pangs of brighter hopes and truer joys. The cloud is often placed to protect from the onslaught of the enemy. God is my reward ... I thank God for difficulties. Make me a man, O God. Live consistently.

> Source: Harold Moody, 'Prize Bible'.

SAM KING (born 1926): Wartime service and friendships
Born in Priestman's River, Jamaica, the son of a farmer, Sam King left school at the age of fifteen. In 1944 he volunteered for the Royal Air Force and arrived in Scotland later that year. King was stationed in various parts of Britain, including at Rivenhall, in Essex, where he became friends with a fellow airman. In late 1947 Sam King returned to Jamaica. (See also p. 147.)

> At Rivenhall, I met Fred Seagraves who took me home to his parents in Bulwell, Nottingham. They were to become my 'English parents' – Mam

and Pap – and I was their black son. The Seagraves had a shop, and whenever I visited them on my days off, my job was to weigh parcels of sugar, rice and flour and make the fire until they arrived from the shop. Because I felt the cold so much, Mam used to put a brick in the coal fire, wrap it in a towel or newspaper and place it between the covers . . .

It had been my intention to remain in the RAF but this was not possible since I had not married an English woman or been selected from Jamaica in the first place for higher education. Having come to terms with the disappointment, I made a farewell visit to Mam and Pap. This was a solemn and grave occasion. Thinking they'd never see their son again, we embraced. Mam threw her arms around me and was profusely tearful.

Source: Sam King, *Climbing Up the Rough Side of the Mountain* (London, 1998), pp. 61–62, 71.

SAM KING: Getting back into church

Sam King was one of the 492 West Indians, mostly men and mainly from Jamaica, who arrived at Tilbury on the *Empire Windrush* in June 1948. He re-enlisted in the RAF and served until 1952. Demobbed, he worked for the Post Office for many years and took an active part in Labour Party politics, becoming a councillor and then the first black mayor of the London borough of Southwark in 1983. Like many of the *Windrush* 'pioneers', King came from a Christian background but found it difficult to identify with, or find both the time and the considerable psychological energy to belong to, a white-run church. As he is reported as saying, 'while many people did not attend church, they did not generally lose their faith'.[8] However, this was to change, and, in this extract from his autobiography, Sam King describes how he became more closely involved in the work of a local black-majority church in south-east London.

One Sunday evening in 1976, I was coming from work when I came face to face with some people, Bibles in hand, in the Herne Hill and Ruskin ward area. Upon enquiry, I discovered that they were meeting in the church hall and the next Sunday I went along to the gathering of nearly a hundred people. I was happy with their style of worship: 'Amen' and

'Praise the Lord' were unbounded. At the end of the service there wasn't a rush for the door; people socialised and the pastor came off the platform and welcomed me heartily.

Source: Sam King, *Climbing Up the Rough Side of the Mountain* (London, 1998), p. 172.

IO SMITH (b. 1951): Coming to 'the Mother Country?'

Io Smith, a pioneer minister in a Pentecostal church, came from Jamaica to Britain in 1957. Her experiences as a black immigrant in Britain were hard. Too often white people find it difficult to understand what black people coming to Britain endured – to be snubbed, insulted, treated with disrespect, all solely because of the colour of their skin. Io Smith's account may open some white eyes!

I was shattered from the first day I arrived ... I had a bedsitter and I hated it. After shutting the door when I got in I felt as if the walls were caving in on me. I had always lived in an open house in Jamaica. The windows were open. When people got up in the morning the doors were opened. Six o'clock in the morning the birds were singing, the sun was shining through the trees, people were, calling out, 'Good morning. How are you?' and stopping for a little chat. The village van was bringing in the bread, buns and cakes.

... When we walked into a shop everybody would turn around to look at us. If we began to speak straightaway they said, 'Pardon me.' I didn't know what all this 'Pardon me' was. Once I went into a shop to buy myself a bottle of vanilla ... The lady said 'Pardon me' about ten times, till I got very embarrassed. She called other people to come over to find what I wanted. Then I spelt it. 'V-A-N-I-L-L-A.' 'Oh,' she said, pronouncing it totally differently. 'Vinelle.'

... I had to accept the habit of drinking tea often because the weather was so cold and it helped to warm me. I couldn't stand gloves and socks and boots. Overcoats. Scarves. Cardigans. Thick jumpers. Warm hats. It was so depressing. The paraffin heater stank. It was even on our clothes when we went out into the streets. And the reception we got on the streets. The type of looks! There were not many black people around and when two or three found themselves in a market place people would actually stand still and turn around and stare. We felt as if we had landed from Mars or somewhere. We didn't understand what was going on. Back home we were part of the community. Here we felt totally strange. It was such a strain for those of us who came in the fifties . . .

Sometimes we would go out for a job and the first thing that would meet our eyes was a notice, 'Sorry. No coloureds.' I can remember going for a job and they just laughed at me, and shut the window . . .

I had to learn to cope with the prejudice, the rejection, the racism that was so very evident. We'd be shouted at, 'Go back.' We were called 'Wogs'. My face was slapped. I felt so rejected and unwanted . . . I've been pushed off the bus, deliberately, by a white conductor . . .

I want to thank God I had faith because in those day, that was the only thing I could turn to. In my despair and loneliness I could always pray. The strength I needed I found through my faith in God. The Bible became more real, more comforting, more of a friend. For many people it was their only consolation. When I first arrived communities were all white. We were so isolated and many of our neighbours, even the people who lived next door, pretended that we weren't there. They said they could not understand us, or we looked like another person they met in the market. If we had more than three visitors they would call it a crowd and ask us in the street how many people lived in the house.

In those days we wouldn't see black people as clerks in the banks or the post offices. We never saw black people as cashiers in the local shops, in Woolworth, or Marks and Spencer's. I used to make it my duty to go into Roman Road market because I would meet a couple of black people there. In the West Indies we didn't have to know people to talk to them. We'd get on the bus, and meet people, and start a conversation. Here people were rushing along, doing their own thing. There was no friendliness. If we could meet a few black people at least we would have someone to talk to.

Source: Io Smith with W. Green, *An Ebony Cross: Being a Black Woman in Britain Today* (London, 1989), pp. 31–39.

Notes

1. The Downs: a semi-sheltered area for sailing ships off the East Kent coast and landward of the treacherous Goodwin Sands.

2. The Greenwich Naval Hospital for sick and injured seamen, in what was then north-west Kent.

3. See above, p. 53, note 2.

4. John Allen, Baptist pastor of a church in Petticoat Lane, Spitalfields, 1764–67.

5. See above, p. 71, note 3.

6. Dogger Bank: a large sandbank in the North Sea.

7. See above, p. 136, note 1.

8. Mark Sturge, *Look What the Lord Has Done! An Exploration of Black Christian Faith in Britain* (Bletchley, 2005), p. 83.

AFTERWORD

Most books and articles written about the history of black people in Britain pay little attention to their religious beliefs. And yet there is no shortage of sources on the lives and experiences of black British Christians. In the late eighteenth century a number of well-known Afro-British writers who were Christians – Equiano, Gronniosaw, and Cugoano – recorded their lives and their hopes in auto-biographies and polemical works. In the next century and a half the number of books and pamphlets written by black men and women and published in Britain increased, and a majority of these were written by Christians. In addition some of their activities were recorded in the growing number of newspapers and magazines that were regularly published. Along with the many weekly religious newspapers, the missionary and church magazines, and the letters and official correspondence generated by those bodies, they all offer a rich store of material to be mined and interpreted. In this way it is possible to get to know more about the experience of black people in Britain.

This book contains only brief passages taken from what a selected number of black men and women wrote or spoke. They have been 'selected' by the compilers because their words were recorded in one way or another, and also because those records or sources were either already known or have been found by research or, as in some cases, by chance. Undoubtedly there are many other black British Christian voices to be discovered, although, of course, the vast majority of people left no record of their lives or of what they believed. Another process of selection has also taken place:

reducing in length many of the accounts included. This has been done to produce a book at a reasonable price, but also because sensible books have the purpose of stimulating curiosity in the reader to want to know more. We hope that this book will do just that, and that readers will want to read more widely and get to know more about black Christians in the past.

In compiling this book much longer texts were collected, from which selections have been made. These longer texts are going to be put on the Set All Free website, <www.setallfree.net/links.html>. The voices and everyday experiences of ordinary people are a vital part of history. Without them our understanding of our collective lives of faith will be reduced, and future generations' knowledge of our age will be diminished.

BIBLIOGRAPHY

Primary sources

Baptist Missionary Society, Angus Library, Regent's College, Oxford, 'Autobiography of the Rev. J. J. Fuller of Cameroons, West Africa', A/5/19.

British Broadcasting Corporation Archives, Caversham, Berkshire, 'Calling the West Indies', BBC broadcast, 2–3 January 1944.

Harold Moody papers, from private collection: Harold Moody, 'My life', ch. 2, 'England', unpublished manuscript; Moody's Bible.

Rhodes House Library, Anti-Slavery Society papers, Oxford, Society for the Propagation of the Gospel in Foreign Parts.

Secondary sources

1. Newspapers and journals, etc.

The African Telegraph.

Anti-Slavery Reporter.

Baptist Register.

Changing London (magazine of the London City Mission).

The Christian Endeavour Times.

Church Missionary Record.

Fraternity.

Illustrated London News.

Jamaica Times.

The Keys (journal of The League of Coloured Peoples).

Lux.

News Letter (of The League of Coloured Peoples).

The Primitive Methodist Magazine for the Year 1829.
Review of Reviews.
The Sword and Trowel (journal of The Pastor's College, London).
Third Way.
The Telephone.

2. Published sources used in the anthology

Barnes, J. Edmestone, *The Signs of the Times Touching the Final Supremacy of Nations* (London, 1903).

Beecham, John, *Ashantee and the Gold Coast* (London, 1841).

Bickersteth, Edward, *Memoir of Simeon Wilhelm A Native of the Susoo Country, West Africa* (New-Haven, 1819).

Boateng, Paul, *Third Way*, April 2004.

Carretta, Vincent, ed., *Phillis Wheatley: Complete Writings* (London, 2001).

Constantine, Learie, *Colour Bar* (London, 1954).

Cugoano, Quobna Ottobah, *Thoughts and Sentiments on the Evil of Slavery* (London, 1787).

Equiano, Olaudah, *The Interesting Narrative of the Life of Olaudah Equiano, or Gustavus Vassa, The African. Written by Himself* (London, 1789; 9th edn, 1794).

George, David, 'An Account of the Life of Mr. David George from Sierra Leone in Africa; given by himself in a Conversation with Brother Rippon of London, and Brother Pearce of Birmingham', in J. Rippon, ed., *The Baptist Annual Register* (1792).

Gronniosaw, Ukawsaw, *A Narrative of the Most Remarkable Particulars in the Life of James Albert Ukawsaw Gronniosaw, An African Prince, as Related by Himself* (Bath, 1772).

Hammon, Briton, *Narrative of the Uncommon Sufferings and Surprising Deliverance of Briton Hammon, A Negro Man, – Servant to General Winslow, of Marshfield, in New-England...* (Boston, 1760).

Hoare, Prince, *The Memoirs of Granville Sharp Esq. Composed from his own Manuscripts*, 2 vols (London, 1828).

Jea, John, *The Life, History and Unparalleled Sufferings of John Jea; The African Preacher. Compiled and Written by Himself* (Portsea, c. 1815).

Jea, John, *A Collection of Hymns. Compiled and Selected by John Jea, African Preacher of the Gospel* (Portsea, 1816).

Johnson, Thomas L., *Twenty-Eight Years a Slave, or the Story of My Life in Three Continents* (1882; 7th edn, Bournemouth, 1909).

King, Boston, 'Memoirs of the Life of Boston King, a Black Preacher. Written by Himself, during his Residence at Kingswood School', *The Methodist Magazine*, March 1798.

King, Sam, *Climbing up the Rough side of the Mountain* (London, 1998).

Marrant, John, *A Narrative of The Lord's wonderful Dealings With John Marrant, A Black (Now Going To Preach the Gospel in Nova-Scotia...) ...* (London, 4th edn, 1785).

McHardie, Elizabeth, and Allan, Andrew, *The Prodigal Continent of Her Prodigal Son and Missionary; or, the Adventures, Conversion and African Labours of Rev. James Newby* (London, 1885).

Merriman-Labor, A. B. C., *Britons Through Negro Spectacles* (London, 1909).

Ocansey, John E., *African Trading; or the trials of William Narh Ocansey* (Liverpool, 1881; new edn ed. by Kwame Arhin, Accra, 1989).

Ordinary of Newgate's, The, *The Ordinary of Newgate, His Account of the Behaviour, Confession, and Dying Words of the Malefactors Who were Executed at Tyburn, 1703–72*.

Plaatje, Sol, *Some of the Legal Disabilities Suffered by the Native Population of the Union of South Africa and Imperial Responsibility* (London, 1919).

Prince, Mary, *The History of Mary Prince, a West Indian Slave* (London, 1831).

Rippon, John, ed., *Annual Baptist Register* (London, 1793).

Roper, Moses, *Narrative of the Adventures and Escapes of Moses Roper, from American Slaver ... with an Appendix Containing the List of Places Visited by the Author in Great Britain and Ireland and the British Isles* (Berwick-upon-Tweed, 1848).

Sancho, Ignatius, *Letters of the Late Ignatius Sancho, An African* (London, 1782; 5th edn, 1803).

Scholes, T. E. S., *Sugar and the West Indies* (London, 1898).

Scholes, T. E. S., *The British Empire and Alliances* (London, 1899).

Scholes, T. E. S., *Glimpses of the Ages or the 'Superior' and 'Inferior' Races, So-called, Discussed in the Light of Science and History*, 2 (London, 1908).

Schön, Frederick, and Crowther, Samuel, *Journals of Rev. James Frederick Schön and Mr. Samuel Crowther* (London, 1842).

Smith, Amanda, *An Autobiography: The Story of the Lord's Dealings with Mrs. Amanda Smith, the Colored Evangelist...* (Chicago, 1893).

Smith, Edwin, *Aggrey of Africa* (London, 1929).

Smith, Io, with Green, W., *An Ebony Cross: Being a Black Woman in Britain Today* (London, 1989).

Smith, John, 'Memoir of Samuel Barber, a local preacher', *The Primitive Methodist Magazine for the Year 1829*, 10.

Stanford, Peter Thomas, *From Bondage to Liberty: Being the life story of the Rev. P. T. Stanford who was once a slave! And is now the recognised pastor of an English Baptist Church* (Smethwick, 1889).

Strickland, S., *Negro Slavery described by A Negro: being The Narrative of Ashton Warner, a Native of St. Vincent* (London, 1831).

Thorne, Albert, 'Tackling a great problem II', *Jamaica Times*, 15 January 1910.

Wheatley, Phillis, *Poems on Various Subjects, Religious and Moral* (London, 1773).

Wilson, Salim, *Jehovah-Nissi: The Life Story of Hatashil-Masha-Kathish of the Dinka Tribe of the Soudan*, 2nd edn (Birmingham, 1901).

Wilson, Salim, *I Was a Slave* (London, n.d., c. 1939).

3. Other printed sources

Adi, Hakim, *West Africans in Britain, 1900–1960* (London, 1998).

Aldred, J. D., *Respect: Understanding Caribbean British Identity* (Peterborough, 2005).

Anderson, Gerald H., ed., *Biographical Dictionary of Christian Missions* (Grand Rapids, 1999).

Anonymous, 'The African Stranger', in the *Cottage Library of Christian Knowledge* (London, n.d., c. 1810).

Anstey, Roger, *The Atlantic Slave Trade and British Abolition 1760–1810* (London, 1975).

Armistead, Wilson, *A Tribute for the Negro* (Manchester, 1848).

Ayres, J., ed., *Paupers and Pig Killers: The Diary of William Holland a Somerset Parson 1799–1818* (Stroud, 1984).

Banton, Michael, *The Coloured Quarter: Negro Immigrants in an English City* (London, 1955).

Beckford, Robert, *Jesus is Dread: Black Theology and Black Culture in Britain* (London, 1998).

Beckford, Robert, *Dread and Pentecostal: A Political Theology for the Black Church in Britain* (London, 2000).

Bernal, Martin, *Black Athena: The Afroasiatic Roots of Classical Civilisation*, 1, 2 (London, 1985, 1991).

Bolt, Christine, *Victorian Attitudes to Race* (London, 1971).

Braidwood, Stephen J., *Black Poor and White Philanthropists: London's Blacks and the Foundation of the Sierra Leone Settlement 1786–1791* (Liverpool, 1994).

Brown, Christopher, 'From slaves to subjects: envisioning an Empire without slavery, 1772–1834', in Philip D. Morgan, and Sean Hawkins, eds., *Black Experience and the Empire* (Oxford, 2005).

Brown, Christopher, *Moral Capital: Foundations of British Abolitionism* (Chapel Hill, NC, 2006).

Carretta, Vincent, ed., *Unchained Voices: An Anthology of Black Authors in the English-Speaking World of the Eighteenth Century* (Lexington, KY, 1996).

Carretta, Vincent, *Equiano the African: Biography of a Self-Made Man* (Athens, GA, 2005).

Christopher, Emma, *Slave Ship Sailors and Their Captive Cargoes, 1730–1807* (Cambridge, 2006).

Colley, Linda, *Captives: Britain, Empire and the World 1600–1850* (London, 2002).

Cromwell, Adelaide M., *An African Woman Feminist: The Life and Times of Adelaide Smith Casely Hayford 1868–1960* (Washington, DC, 1992).

Cugoano, Quobna Ottobah, *Thoughts and Sentiments on the Evil of Slavery*, ed. Vincent Carretta (London, 1999).

Curtin, Philip, ed., *Africa Remembered: Narratives by West Africans from the Era of the Slave Trade* (Madison, WI, 1968).

Curtin, Philip, *The Image of Africa: British Ideas and Action, 1780–1850* (London, 1965).

Dabydeen, David, Gilmore, John, and Jones, Cecily, eds., *Oxford Companion to Black British History* (Oxford, 2007).

Dabydeen, David, and Rewt, Polly, eds., *The Letters of Ignatius Sancho* (Edinburgh, 1994).

Davis, David A., Evans, Tampathia, Finseth, Ian Frederick, and Williams, Andrea N., eds., *North Carolina Slave Narratives: The Lives of Moses Roper, Lunsford Lane, Moses Grandy and Thomas H. Jones* (Chapel Hill, NC, 2005).

Davis, David Brion, *The Problem of Slavery in the Age of Revolution 1770–1823* (Oxford, 1975).

Davis, Robert C., *Christian Slaves and Muslim Masters: White Slavery in the Mediterranean, The Barbary Coast and Italy, 1500–1800* (Basingstoke, 2003).

Debrunner, H. W., *Presence and Prestige: Africans in Europe: A History of Africans in Europe Before 1918* (Basel, 1979).

Edwards, Paul, and Walvin, James, *Black Personalities in the Era of the Slave Trade* (London, 1983).

Erlmann, Veit, *Music, Modernity, and the Global Imagination: South Africa and the West* (New York, 1999).

Frost, Diane, *Work and Community Among West African Migrant Workers Since the Nineteenth Century* (Liverpool, 1999).

Fryer, Peter, *Staying Power: The History of Black People in Britain* (London, 1984).

Fyfe, Christopher, ed., *Our Children Free and Happy: Letters from Black Settlers in Africa in the 1790s* (Edinburgh, 1991).

Fyfe, Christopher, 'Sierra Leoneans in English schools in the nineteenth century', in Rainer Lotz and Ian Pegg, eds., *Under the Imperial Carpet: Essays in Black History 1780–1950* (Crawley, 1986).

Geiss, Imanuel, *The Pan-African Movement* (London, 1974).

Gerzina, Gretchen Holbrook, *Black England: Life Before Emancipation* (London, 1995).

Gerzina, Gretchen Holbrook, *Black Victorians/Black Victoriana* (New Brunswick, NJ, 2003).

Gordon, Grant, *From Slavery to Freedom: The Life of David George, Pioneer Black Baptist Minister* (Nova Scotia, 1992).

Green, Jeffrey, 'John Alcindor (1873–1924): a migrant's biography', *Immigrants and Minorities* 6.2 (1987).

Green, Jeffrey, *Black Edwardians: Black People in Britain 1901–1914* (London, 1998).

Grosvenor, Ian, McLean, Rita, and Roberts, Siân, eds., *Making Connections: Birmingham Black International History* (Birmingham, 2002).

Gundara, Jagdish S., and Duffield, Ian, eds., *Essays on the History of Blacks in Britain* (Aldershot, 1992).

Hall, Catherine, *Civilising Subjects: Metropole and Colony in the English Imagination* (Oxford, 2002).

Hargreaves, John D., 'The Good Black Doctor: Christopher J. Davis, 1840–1870', *ASACHIB Newsletter* 16 (1996), pp. 6–7.

Hill, Robert A., 'Zion on the Zambesi: Dr J. Albert Thorne, "A Descendant of Africa and Barbados", and the African colonial enterprise: The "preliminary stage", 1894–7', in Jagdish S. Gundara and Ian Duffield, eds., *Essays on the History of Blacks in Britain* (Aldershot, 1992), pp. 99–123.

Hodges, Graham Russell (ed.), *Black Itinerants of the Gospel: The Narratives of John Jea and George White* (New York, 1993).

Hofmeyr, Isabel, *The Portable Bunyan: A Transnational History of The Pilgrim's Progress* (Princeton, NJ, 2004).

Howe, Stephen, *Afrocentrism: Mythical Pasts and Imagined Homes* (London, 1998).

James, Winston, 'The Black experience in twentieth-century Britain', in Philip D. Morgan and Sean Hawkins, eds., *Black Experience and the Empire* (Oxford, 2004), pp. 347–386.

Jekyll, Joseph, *Letters of the Late Ignatius Sancho* (London, 1968).

Jenkins, Ray, 'Gold Coasters overseas, 1880–1919: with specific reference to their activities in Britain', *Immigrants and Minorities* 4.3, (1985), pp. 5–25.

Jenkinson, Jacqueline, 'The 1919 race riots in Britain: a survey', in Rainer Lotz and Ian Pegg, eds., *Under the Imperial Carpet: Essays in Black History 1780–1950* (Crawley, 1986), pp. 182–207.

Kaufman, Miranda, ' "The speedy transportation of blackamoores": Caspar Van Senden's search for Africans and profit in Elizabethan England', *Black and Asian Studies Association Newsletter* 45 (April 2006), pp. 10–14.

Killingray, David, ed., *Africans in Britain* (London, 1994).

Killingray, David, 'The Black Atlantic missionary movement and Africa, 1780s–1920s', *Journal of Religion in Africa* 33.1 (2003), pp. 3–31.

Killingray, David, 'Black Baptists in Britain 1640–1950', *Baptist Quarterly* 40 (April 2003), pp. 69–89.

Killingray, David, ' "All conditions of life and labour": The presence of Black people in Essex before 1950', *Essex Archaeology and History* 35 (2004), pp. 114–122.

Killingray, David, 'Black evangelicals in darkest Britain, 1780s–1930s', in Mark Smith, ed., *British Evangelical Identities: Past, Present and Possible Futures*, 1: *History and Sociology* (Carlisle, 2007).

Killingray, David, ' "To do something for the race": Harold Moody and the League of Coloured Peoples', in Bill Schwarz, ed., *West Indian Intellectuals in Britain* (Manchester, 2003), pp. 51–70.

King, Reyahn *et al.*, *Ignatius Sancho: An African Man of Letters* (London, 1997).

Klein, Herbert S., *The Atlantic Slave Trade* (Cambridge, 1999).

Lawless, Richard I., *From Ta'izz to Tyneside: An Arab Community in the North-East During the Early Twentieth Century* (Exeter, 1995).

Little, Kenneth, *Negroes in Britain: A Study of Racial Relations in English Society* (London, 1972).

Llywd, Alan, *Cymru Ddu Black Wales: A History* (Cardiff, 2005).

Lotz, Rainer and Pegg, Ian, eds., *Under the Imperial Carpet: Essays in Black History 1780–1950* (Crawley, 1986).

Lorimer, Douglas A., *Colour, Class and the Victorians: English Attitudes to the Negro in the Mid-Nineteenth Century* (Leicester, 1978).

Macdonald, Roderick, 'Dr. Harold Moody and the League of Coloured People, 1931–1947: a retrospective view', *Race* 14.3 (1975), pp. 291–310.

Marsh, Jan, ed., *Black Victorians: Black people in British Art 1800–1900* (Aldershot, 2005).

Matthew, Colin, and Harrison, John, eds., *Oxford Dictionary of National Biography* (Oxford, 2004).

McCalman, Iain, ed., *The Horrors of Slavery and Other Writings by Robert Wedderburn* (Edinburgh, 1991).

Milton, Gilles, *White Gold: The Extraordinary Story of Thomas Pellow and North Africa's One Million European Slaves* (London, 2004).

Myers, Norma, 'Servant, sailor, soldier, tailor, beggerman: black survival in white society 1780–1830', *Immigrants and Minorities* 12.1 (1993), pp. 47–74.

Myers, Norma, *Reconstructing the Past: Blacks in Britain 1780–1830* (London, 1996).

Nash, Gary B., *The Forgotten Fifth: African Americans in the Age of Revolution* (Cambridge, MA, 2006).

Perham, Margery, ed., *Ten Africans: A Collection of Life Stories* (London, 1936).

Potkay, Adam, and Burr, Sandra, eds., *Black Atlantic Writers of the Eighteenth Century: Living the New Exodus in England and the Americas* (Basingstoke, 1995).

Rich, Paul, *Race and Empire in British Politics* (Cambridge, 1990).

Richmond, Legh, *Annals of the Poor: The Negro Servant* (London, c. 1809).

Salih, Sara, ed., *Mary Prince: The History of Mary Prince* (London, 2000).

Schneer, Jonathan, *London 1900: The Imperial Metropolis* (London, 1999).

Scobie, Edward, *Black Britannia: A History of Blacks in Britain* (Chicago, 1972).

Sherwood, Marika, *Pastor Daniels Ekarte and the African Churches Mission* (London, 1994).

Shyllon, Folarin, *Black Slaves in Britain* (Oxford, 1974).

Shyllon, Folarin, *Black People in Britain 1555–1833* (Oxford, 1977).

Sparks, Randy J., *The Two Princes of Calabar: An Eighteenth-Century Atlantic Odyssey* (Cambridge, MA, 2004).

Spencer, Ian R. G., *British Immigration Policy Since 1939: The Making of Multi-Racial Britain* (London, 1997).

Sturge, Mark, *Look What the Lord Has Done! An Exploration of Black Christian Faith in Britain* (Bletchley, 2005).

Thomas, Hugh, *The Slave Trade: The Story of the Atlantic Slave Trade 1440–1870* (London, 1997).

Walvin, James, *Black and White: The Negro and English Society 1555–1945* (London, 1973).

Walvin, James, *England, Slaves and Freedom, 1776–1838* (Basingstoke, 1986).

Walvin, James, *Black Ivory: A History of British Slavery* (London, 1992).

Walvin, James, *An African's Life: The Life and Times of Olaudah Equiano, 1745–1797* (London, 1998).

West, Shearer, *The Victorians and Race* (Leicester, 1996).

Whyte, Iain, *Scotland and the Abolition of Black Slavery 1756–1838* (Edinburgh, 2006).

Willan, Brian, *Sol Plaatje: South African Nationalist 1876–1932* (London, 1984).

Willan, Brian, ed., *Sol Plaatje: Selected Writings* (Johannesburg, 1996).

Wise, Steven M., *Though the Heavens May Fall: The Landmark Trial That Led to the End of Human Slavery* (Cambridge, MA, 2005).

Woodson, Carter G., *The Mind of the Negro as Reflected in Letters During the Crisis, 1800–1860* (Washington, DC, 1926).

Yorke, Philip C., ed., *The Diary of John Baker* (London, 1931).

Unpublished theses

Chater, Kathy, 'Untold Histories: Black People in England During the British Slave Trade, 1660–1807' (PhD thesis, University of London, forthcoming).

Walker, Paul, 'The Reverend Peter Thomas Stanford (1860–1909): Birmingham's "Coloured Preacher"' (PhD thesis, Manchester University, 2004).

INDEX